Harry Reardon is a qualified lawyer who, at the age of thirty-one, left the law completely to train as a sports journalist. He now works in the civil service. He lives in a small village outside Winchester with his wife and their two young children.

How To Be An Olympian

How To Be An Olympian

Harry Reardon

unbound

This edition first published in 2021

Unbound

TC Group, Level 1, Devonshire House, One Mayfair Place
London W1J 8AJ

www.unbound.com

ISBN (eBook): 978-1-78965-102-7

ISBN (Paperback): 978-1-78965-101-0

Cover design by Mecob

Printed and bound in Great Britain by Clays Ltd, Elcograf S.p.A.

For Dad

Super Patrons

Emmaline Achilles
Gideon Achilles
Rehan Ahmed
Anneliese Allen-Norris
Natasha Animashaun
Mark Bailey
Jonathan Barker
Jennifer Bhatt
Michelle Brookes
Chris Brophy
Euan Burns
Freddie Capper
Tim Clark
Jenny Collins
Ian Cooper
DailyDOOH Cotterill
Andrew Craig
James Cushing
Thomas Dance
Michael Darling
Natalie Deffenbaugh

Hiren Dhimar
Claire Eadington
Pauline Edwards
Simon Edwards
Marlon EL-Moor
Esther Evans
Rebecca Fairclough
Tony Fallows
Jeff Farnworth
Martha Farnworth
Peter Fellows
Jonathan Gilbert
Fiona Goodall
Martin Gough
Rosalind Green
Matthew Hamilton
Sarah Hankey
Nick Harvey
Chris Hurst
Savannah & Leonie Keefe
Laura Leach
Justin Leese
Tim Lewis
Katie Meadows
Adam Morallee
Edward Moss
Olga Mykhalets
Victoria Nowell
Aoife O'Leary
Jo Pickersgill
Rebecca Pike
Gregory Price
Joanna Price

Mabel Price
Magnus Price
Mr Pugs
Jessica Randall-Carrick
Annette Reardon
Helen Reardon
Stephanie Reardon Streetz
Francesca Rhodes
David Richardson
Rob Ritchie
Mark Rogers
Anne Marie Rugeris
David Rutterford
Margaret Rutterford
Rebecca Seibel
Shakira Shute
Victoria Slack
Robert Stanier
John Tippett-Cooper
Diane Umpleby
James Umpleby
Mike Umpleby
Harry Weir
Paul Wing
Nigel Wissett-Warner
Freya Woods
David Worrall

Contents

The Start

There's an old joke about a tourist who gets lost in the countryside. After wandering around aimlessly for a while, she stumbles across a farmer, and she asks him for directions into town.

"Well," replies the farmer, after a long pause. "I wouldn't start from here."

*

"I'M GONNA QUIT"

If you ever find yourself booking a room at the Crowne Plaza Hotel in Reading – and the *Rough Guide to Berkshire* this isn't, but one never knows when the urge may take hold – make sure you ask for one round the back.

This is important. Otherwise, when your alarm goes off too early of a morning, and you lever yourself out of bed, grumble your way to the kettle and then potter across to the window to open the curtains and take in the day, if you're lucky there's going to be a tree in your face. If not, reading from right to left, it's petrol station, greasy spoon, redbrick office, roundabout. A greasy spoon with a solid set of TripAdvisor reviews it may be, and doubtless plenty of the employees of the Reading branch of Peter Brett Associates are more than content with their life choices, but none of that changes the fact that this is not the view they advertise on the hotel website.

So drink your tea. Head downstairs, manoeuvre your way past the spreadsheet printouts and meal time notices pinned to the whiteboard in the foyer, and press on through the café, because once you make it out of the glass doors at the back and onto the terrace, suddenly there is late summer sunlight twinkling off the Thames. The birds are singing, the sky is an impudent blue, and it's a different world.

It's all so serene, so far removed from the hammering heart of built-up Britain that's beating no more than a hundred yards away, so gently perfect, that if this weren't August 2016, you'd expect Jess Leyden to be feeling pretty well-disposed towards it. But it is, and so she isn't.

She perches uncomfortably on a rickety metal chair, her knees hunched up to her chest. "You look at some of them," she says. "And you say, well, why can't I do that?"

Jess has been watching a lot of telly recently. Team mates, roommates, former crew mates, friends and rivals have been out in Rio de Janeiro over the last couple of weeks, competing at an Olympic Games. They've been breaking records and they've been winning medals, and she could have been there too.

She's got the talent. Everyone at British Rowing knows it, and has done for a few years now, ever since she won the country's first ever international gold medal in the women's single scull[1], at the 2013 World Junior Championships out in Lithuania. But the quadruple scull she's been in for her two seasons in the senior squad missed out on Olympic qualification, and so here she is. Everyone else, it seems, is over in Brazil, and she's sitting outside a hotel in the Home Counties and reliving the moment, three months earlier at the final qualification regatta, when a crew made up of her, Holly Nixon, Ro Bradbury and Tina Stiller finished behind China, Ukraine and New Zealand and fell five seconds short of Rio.

"After we missed out, I didn't know what to do," she says. "I knew we would have to do something quite special at that regatta, but in that moment I really believed we could. We had a good platform, we knew how we could get faster, and it was slowly getting there. But if you're a crew like we were, who were really fighting for the places, you're affected more. You change your tactics more than an established crew would. Maybe that's wrong."

---

1. There are two types of rowing, sculling and sweep, with the difference being, in essence, that scullers get two oars each. Jess has always been a sculler, mainly because when she first took up the sport, at Hollingworth Lake Rowing Club on the outskirts of Rochdale, there was rarely anyone else of her age around for her to row with. Given that you only have one oar if you're doing sweep, if it's just you in the boat then either you're going to end up going round in circles, or it's going to be a canoe.

There was one thing for certain – she wasn't going to leave the sport. She might still be so new to the national team set-up that she doesn't even think of herself as a rower – "I don't really feel like I've grown up. I feel like I'm still doing my hobby" – and she might only have turned down a place at Newcastle University two years ago, on the basis that she'd just made it into the Great Britain senior squad, and it's easier for an international rower to become an engineer than it is for an engineer to become an international rower. But unlike in 2012, when Jess was still splashing about in the junior ranks and the team that dominated at Dorney was becoming the stuff of legend – now, she knows she's good enough. She's got the numbers on the rowing machines, and she's proving herself on the water. Now, she needs to keep sharpening up her technique. She needs to stay fit, and she needs to find the boat that will take her to Tokyo.

First up, a hop over the North Sea to Rotterdam, and the Under-23 World Championships. Since the quad missed out on the Olympics, the coaches have been lining Jess up for a double with the other stand-out sculling prospect in the British women's squad, Mathilda Hodgkins-Byrne. It's a boat, though, that has no history and very possibly no future, however well they perform. It's not nothing, of course – it'll keep them in shape, it might well earn them a medal. But it's been cobbled together at short notice essentially to give them both something to do, and age-group racing in the September of an Olympic year is not why either of them got into the sport.

For Jess and Mathilda, what the next few months are really about is getting in the best possible shape for trials – the series of head-to-head races, time trials and rowing machine tests which runs between November and April each year, punctuating the punishing winter-to-spring training programme. It's a gruelling experience, which will officially form the basis for crew selections for next season and in practice quite probably beyond; in fact, it's fair to say that what happens at the upcoming final assessment, in April next year, could end up defining the whole Olympic cycle. Which makes it important, obviously, even if it probably doesn't help to think of it like that.

"Sometimes people—" begins Jess, and she names no names, but that's not the point, this could be anyone, any sport, any cycle, any country – "...sometimes people get really caught up in trials, and trying to be the best person in the country. Whereas actually, in day-to-day training as a team, you should be thinking about beating the world. That's the team I want to be a part of, a strong team that wants to beat the world and not just each other, that shouts to each other to get better, but that supports each other, and doesn't tear each other down. Because you'd rather miss out on a team that's winning a gold medal than be in a team that comes last."

Team dynamics. At the very top level, a huge amount of sport is about how to get people working together, and it's a tricky business. For one thing, assuming Jess makes it into a boat this time around, it's going to be completely different to the one that missed out on Rio, not least because over the next few weeks, half of the old crew will quit the squad – Ro to try her hand at cycling, Tina to turn her back on professional sport entirely and join Deloitte. So if there is going to be a return to the quad – and Jess admits to a feeling of unfinished business – there will need to be new team mates, new relationships. The only one left from the previous cycle that she could be racing alongside is Holly Nixon, and the two of them haven't always seen eye-to-eye.

"When we first came onto the team together, we didn't really trust each other," says Jess. "I think Holly had a few issues outside of training that she was trying to work through, but she was quite closed about those. Whereas with my personality, I'm a bit of a bull in a china shop." But then British Rowing brought in someone from one of those companies that do team insight profiles, the upshot of which was everyone on the squad being assigned colours to represent their personalities. Holly came out as Earth Green, Jess was a Fiery Red, and just like that, it started to make a bit more sense. So now when Jess blurts out something critical, Holly knows that she's not doing it to upset her, and when Holly is acting all sensitive and over-thinking things, it's not because she wants to piss Jess off. It's anyone's guess how that will play out in the long term if they end up back in a boat together, but for now it's great, it's lovely, it's Junior and Yul at the end of *Cool Runnings*. Holly helps Jess rein herself in, and if Jess really believes in what she's saying, she'll explain why and they'll talk it through, and now Holly's one of the closest friends Jess has got.

The double with Mathilda takes the gold medal with a bit to spare, which if practically inconsequential is still pretty sweet. It comes at the cost of injuries to Jess's rib and back, though, so when the squad's annual three-week break comes around in October, she decides that she really needs to make the most of it. She had planned to go on a walking holiday, but the injuries put paid to that, so it becomes a chance to go home, see her mother and catch up with friends for a bit. Then it's straight back to the team's base in Caversham, just upriver from the Crowne Plaza, and back into the grind.

It starts as a six day week. From Monday to Wednesday, the team gets switched around between crew boats – eights and quads mainly – and then from Thursday to Saturday, they're in their singles. Jess, who's been spending a lot of time in the quad, has been going out for Sunday morning bike rides as well, which she shouldn't really be doing – but then it would be rude not to, she says, the weather's been so pleasant. Then, as the weeks go on and trials get closer, there'll be more and more singles work, and the mileage will start to ratchet up.

She'll also be competing in a four-way invitational exhibition race on the Thames called the Wingfield Sculls. In itself, it's meaningless. It's not part of the training programme, and times posted and victories achieved will count for nothing four years down the line. But since the women's version of the race was revived in 2007 following a 30-odd year hiatus the reasons for which are simultaneously both slightly unclear and shamefully self-apparent, London 2012 gold medallists Anna Watkins and Sophie Hosking have both won it; so has double Olympian Beth Rodford, and so too Rio silver medallist Melanie Wilson and double Olympic bronze medallist Elise Laverick. Barcelona gold medallist Greg Searle has won the men's race, and so has London bronze medallist Alan Campbell, so too double Olympic gold medallist Mahé Drysdale, and back in the 1980s there were five wins in a row for that fella who used to paddle with Pinsent. The bottom line is that it's a serious honour even to be asked to compete, and when Jess wins, against GB team mate Georgia Francis and former squad members Amelia Carlton and Pippa Whittaker, she's suddenly got a lot to live up to.

And so she keeps on pushing, in the gym and on the water. She's pushing so hard, in fact, that she makes herself ill, and misses the first round of trials in November. She's ill in December too, when the next round comes along, but she won't admit it to the team doctor, and so she drags herself up the course a couple of times and somehow finishes second, behind Mathilda.

And autumn gives way to winter.

One by one they come, along the road to Randa, cresting the hill and pushing on up to the monastery; and then one by one, they burst into tears. There are European champions here, world champions, Olympic medallists. One of them, a veteran of Rio, sits almost silent on a bench over to one side, stirring only to tell herself and anyone who will listen, "I'm gonna quit, I'm gonna quit." It's been a relentless climb, hour upon hour in the heat on a bumpy road, and these women might be supremely fit, strong-willed to a fault, hard-wired to take the pain and come back asking for more, but they're not built for cycling.

It's the new year. Everyone's had a bit of a break – home on the afternoon of 23rd December, back at base for 2nd January – although perhaps "break", conveying as it does images of feet up, TV on, mulled wine in one hand and mince pie in the other, isn't quite the word. Instead, your elite rower is training, every day other than New Year's Day and Christmas, two sessions a day in a combination of weights and time on the rowing machine.

There are different ways of going about that. Some people go to a gym near home (if they apply through the British Olympic Association, they can join for free), some take an ergo[2] away with them, but Jess just goes back to her old rowing club, Hollingworth Lake. It's nice to catch up with everyone, she says, even if in truth there aren't quite so many familiar faces any more. There's a few of her former coaches as well as some of the older members, but most of the people that were Jess's age are now at university or have jobs, and they don't row

---

2. Short for ergometer, which is technically defined as an apparatus for measuring the effort that someone's putting in while they exercise. In practice, though, the word "ergo" – or "erg", if you're super busy and don't have time for the final o – is synonymous with "rowing machine".

so much these days. One or two come back for Christmas, but they're not the ones doing 16km ergo sessions topped off with some weights work, or a 5k with a mid-session rate change.

Every few days, Jess sends her 30 minute ergo scores and her 5k times back to her coaches, and she's keeping a log of her weights work too; and then when she gets back, it's straight into the training camps. Usually there would have been one before Christmas too, but not this year, with the post-Olympics upheaval of retirements and new arrivals. So the first camp of the 2017 season takes place in early January – a fortnight at a base just outside the little Portuguese town of Avis, before a brief spell at home is followed by a couple of weeks in Majorca. After another stop-off back in the UK, it'll be overseas again to squeeze in another camp before the racing starts; but for now, as February turns to March, here they are in the Balearics, and on the road to Randa.

It's been a constant incline, with a steep hill right at the end before they reach the monastery, so adding in the headwind into which they've been riding pretty much the entire time, it's taken about three hours. Jess has been riding alongside a couple of others and they've said next to nothing to each other all the way, it's that exhausting. Finally they make it up to the top, to the place where they're going to have lunch, and everyone is just silent except the Rio veteran, who's slumped on the bench telling Jess how much more fun she could be having with her life.

Jess gets a bit ill again, obviously, that's what mile after mile of cycling day after day, plus weights plus maybe an 18km ergo run will do to you; but she manages to ease off on a few things, and doesn't end up missing much. And she's there for Sa Calobra.

If there is such a thing as the perfect cycling climb, Sa Calobra might well be it. For those with the strength to lift their heads, it offers spectacular views over the Mediterranean; for the rider whose attention is drawn more downwards than out, the road packs a full coiffure of hairpins. There's a section where the overhanging rocks have collapsed together and it feels almost like you're riding through a cathedral, and one part where the road turns back on itself so much that it becomes its own bridge. The route snakes upwards at a steady pace, but with a couple of sharp upticks so you can't just churn over and switch off. It's not so easy as to be of no interest to the professionals – as of early 2017, the leaderboard on Strava is peppered with names from the top of the cycling world, from Simon Yates to Emma Pooley, Clara Koppenburg to Sebastián Henao – but it's not too hard for amateurs either. And it's quirky – the road to the summit is the only way out of the port at the bottom that lends the climb its name, so before you haul your way up it, first you've got to hurtle down.

"We set off one-by-one and time trial," explains Jess. "It's a 600-metre-odd climb[3], 9km from bottom to top, and it takes about 40 minutes. And then you turn around at the top, go back down, do the climb again, and then ride two hours home." At least, that was the plan. Because she's been ill, she's only allowed to climb it once. So she gives it everything she's got, and winds up completing it quicker than any open weight[4] female GB rower has ever done before. Which is nice.

So all in all, it's a good camp, something which Paul Thompson, the head coach for the women's squad, recognises after the final 30 minute ergo. Still not at a hundred per cent, Jess doesn't post great numbers, but he's been watching, and at the end he nods, and tells her that he thinks she's got the most out of it that

---

3. 668m, if you're going for the Strava segment.
4. Rowing offers a few lightweight racing categories, in which competitors have to be below a certain weight in order to compete. Open weight boats have no such restrictions.

she could. He compliments her on her camp performance and how she's developing as an athlete, and she starts to think yeah, maybe I'm doing okay.

And then, just while things seem to be ticking along smoothly on the water, Jess breaks her phone. On the way back from Majorca, she leaves her laptop in airport security, and when she gets home, it's to a car that has been clamped after she forgot to pay her tax. What's more, she's come to realise that she will have to defer the engineering degree she's doing part time with the Open University, because she's been struggling with time management around the assessments, and frankly, things have been getting a bit on top of her. And so she does what any sensible person would do in the circumstances, and she rings her mum to tell her that she feels like she's been failing as an adult.

And her mum, as mothers do, tells her that she's being an idiot, and that everything will be fine.

*

SILENCE ON THE WHATSAPP GROUP

"You can do all your training perfectly. You can do extra sessions. But then you could be over-training – those extra sessions could actually be detrimental. And then even if you train at just the right intensity, at just the right amount of each intensity, you could have someone else who did their training perfectly too, and just has a better physiology. Or maybe you crack under pressure.

"Then there's the conditions. Perhaps you're not very good at sculling in rough water and you catch a blade three more times than the other boat, and that loses you three tenths of a second. The bottom line is that it's not as simple as doing more sessions, or just having a really good attitude throughout your training, because then it would be predictable. And that's why it's fun."

Down on the start line in Belgrade, though, it doesn't look too much like fun. At stroke sits Jess, staring through the rain that's beginning to sheet down around her. Behind her at seat three, Holly Nixon is back in the boat; Beth Bryan, a 24-year-old Teessider who came to rowing in her teens after a promising junior swimming career, is at two; and finally, at bow, comes Mathilda.

It's the first world cup of the season. But the name notwithstanding, world cups – of which there are three every year – don't actually count for much, especially this far ahead of the Olympics, so there hasn't been a great deal of interest from the other nations. None at all, in fact, apart from Poland and the Netherlands. So it's going to be a three-boat race; and what's more, it's going to be a three-boat race in which the GB quadruple scull won't be finishing in the top two. Both the Poles and the Dutch were in the medals at Rio, and both countries have two members of those crews returning for this first race of the new cycle. But if destiny dictates that the journey to Tokyo gold is going to start with coming last in the Serbian rain – then so be it.

Here we are again then, having another crack at the quad. After another camp, this time in Italy's Varese, and another exhibition race – the 80-odd-year-old Women's Eights Head of the River – the final weekend of trials for the 2017 season came along in April with, *mirabile dictu*, Jess at more or less full fitness. It's far from unusual to struggle with illness and injury over the trials period – Beth hadn't made it to an assessment since November, and last year Zoë Lee, who ended up stroking the Rio eight to silver, managed to miss the lot of them as well as all the ergo tests; but that's just the way it goes.

In fact, to get the best out of yourself at trials, it probably helps to start from outside the squad, because then you can properly taper your training. If you're already part of the set-up, you'll have been doing big training blocks for a while, and what's more won't be quite so inclined to pull yourself up when you start feeling under the weather. Of course, all of that should then be taken into account by the coaching staff when it comes to selection. That, at least, is the theory.

In the event, most people made it to the big dénouement, and it all went broadly to form. Vicky Thornley, coming back after Rio and the retirement of double sculls crew mate Katherine Grainger in the hope of proving herself in a single, pulled out in front in the final race and managed to hold off a rapidly closing Jess; Mathilda, having jumped out early but blown up, finished third, and Beth followed in not far behind. The trials winner traditionally gets asked whether or not they want to do the single, so Vicky took it, although Jess says that she wouldn't have fancied it even if she'd won. She'd been doing a lot of work in the quad over the winter, with Holly and Mathilda and a rotating cast of fourth members, and she has high hopes.

"We've got some seriously strong girls, and we've got unfinished business in the quad. I really, really wanted to do it," she says. "I think we can do well. Obviously it would be good if we could have Vicky in it, but if she wants to do the single, then she wouldn't necessarily be as invested in the quad's project.

"And we're excited. We're all a similar age, we're all young – I actually came up through juniors with Beth and Mathilda. So while I didn't get a choice about boats as such, as a group we've made it quite clear from the beginning of the year that we wanted to do the quad. And in the Avis camp, we were going really fast, so I think it's got promise."

Belgrade is the crew's first race together, and Jess is at stroke. She hasn't asked why. The plan seems to be to change things up throughout the season, see what works and what doesn't. In the long term, though, they'll need to pick some arrangement and stick to it, because each seat needs different skills. Stroke, for instance, is the boat's heartbeat, setting up the rhythm, tapping out the steps of the dance. Three, who's sat immediately behind her, has a part to play in that too, but also has to bring raw power and hard work, as does two. Two does most of the calls and generally takes a bit more control of the boat, and then there's bow, who has to be right up with stroke, almost anticipating the catch, and so needs the sharpest technique of them all.

So where would Jess put herself, if she had the choice? Diplomacy ("it depends who I'm rowing with") gives way to an admission that she's not particularly enjoying stroke, "because I'm a bit of a control freak"; and then she ponders for a moment. "I'd quite like to be at two. I feel like at two you really set the tone for each outing. You're trying to feel the boat and you're basically telling everyone what to do. Also, I've been at two the past two years. I've learnt a lot about that seat, and I think I'd quite like to have a bit more say over how we're approaching things. But I've got to learn to let other people do their thing as well, I suppose." There's those team dynamics again. Zip it, Fiery Red.

It feels like they'll need to nail it down soon enough for the good of the boat, but for now at least there's an argument that switching seats means a chance to learn more about the rest of the crew. You have a bit more understanding for the people that are in each of the seats, why they say the things they do. "Bow of a quad," says Jess, "feels completely different to stroke. You feel different things in the boat. Like, it's faster at bow. I know that sounds a bit stupid, because you're in the same boat, but it feels a bit lighter, which means that you've got to be more agile."

There will be two races in Serbia – a heat, which with there being only three entries will solely determine lane order, and then the final. In the heat, it's third place by a distance; in the final, Poland disappear up the water from the gun, and then the Netherlands pull away for silver. So it's a bronze for GB. It's the first medal for a women's quad at a senior international event since before London 2012; on the other hand, it's also finishing last, twice. And if that's about what they expected in terms of result, it's not what they were hoping for in terms of performance. "We underperformed massively," says Jess. "We got a bit tight, we didn't move well together."

Why? They'd been producing good speed in some of their training runs, racking up the numbers at lower stroke rates, but in the race, they'd seized up. They'd tried to force the pace rather than letting the boat do more of the work, and allowing it to run further between strokes. So the next ten days or so of training before the European Championships in Račice, in the Czech Republic – competition comes thick and fast during the racing season – will be all about rhythm, timing, accuracy, patience.

But how to measure that? There are numbers, of course, lots of numbers, most of them coming from a little box inside the boat which the crew knows as "the biomech", and which measures the force going into the blades, the boat's velocity, its acceleration, all sorts. The numbers it spits out get broken down into a little session summary booklet, which the coach will turn into pointers for the crew; but the problem doesn't seem to be coming through there. As far as the biomech is concerned, things are looking good. Maybe that adds to the growing sense of frustration within the boat, and leads to their first big bust-up.

Tensions had been building even before Belgrade, and at a meeting shortly after they get back, Holly snaps. She gets angry in a way that she's never really done before in front of the crew, calls Jess aggressive, which Jess finds hard to take, and both of them end up upset. A quad isn't like a double, where there's no-one else to patch things up after a fight, and the whole thing can just fall apart. But then it's not the same as an eight either, where if things get too heated, you can just move someone from one end of the boat to the other. So the problem simmers – on the water, they're trying to put things aside, but outside of training, the coffee meetings stop. No popping by each other's houses of an evening. Silence on the WhatsApp group.

Holly in particular is still affected when the Europeans come around, despite the best efforts of Mathilda and Beth to push her and Jess back together. What's more, there's suddenly a much bigger – and better – field of competitors. The Poles bring in another of their Rio bronze medal-winning crew, while the Dutch draft in a couple of veterans from the eight that finished sixth in Brazil, to leave themselves with a boatful of Olympians. Ukraine has entered a boat, containing three of the crew that took fourth place at the Olympics. And then there's Germany – the reigning Olympic champions, winners of three out of the last four Europeans, possessors of the world record women's quad time. They've brought in a completely new crew, but – well, they're the Germans.

And GB beat them.

In the heats, at least. It's a fine performance – even leaving something in the tank, they manage to knock Germany back into third and into the repêchage[5]. They've switched the order in the boat, putting Holly at stroke, Beth at bow, and moving Jess and Mathilda to the engine room; and on Jess's account of the changes, it seems a bit of a surprise that they hadn't done it earlier. "Mathilda's really good at calling," she explains, "which is important at two, and Beth was always at bow when she used to be in the eight. And in the stroke seat, I was finding it really hard." So there it is.

The final is pretty impressive too, although they're struggling a bit with the start. "Our first ten strokes aren't that

---

5. Rowing, unlike most other civilised sports, lacks the courtesy to simply let you lose in the first round and go home. The exact arrangements will depend on how many boats have entered the regatta, but as long as there's a fair few, it's going to go something like this. If, in your opening heat, you finish outside the automatic qualification places for the next round, then you race again in the repêchage, up against the other boats that missed out too. If you don't pick up one of the extra qualification places they give out in that, you're *still* going to have to race again, because rowing doesn't just do finals, either. It does 'A' finals, for the top six boats; then 'B' finals, for the next six, and so on until they've run out of boats, and if the total number of entries isn't nicely divisible by six, then if they can, they'll race you anyway. So if you're, say, Libya's Alhussein Ghambour, and you're the weakest of the 32 entrants in the men's single sculls at Rio 2016, you're damn well going to have to prove it by losing a two-man F final to Vladislav Yakovlev of Kazakhstan, sunshine.

bad," says Jess. "We've got raw power. But because we're so tense and tight, we're not technically as sharp as everyone else, and that affects our second ten strokes, when everyone just moves away from us." Sure enough, the Germans, after sailing through the repêchage, do just that in the final, and despite late pushes from the Dutch and a fast-finishing GB, they hold on for yet another European gold.

But if it's another bronze for Britain this time, it's a much better one than Belgrade. It makes a difference within the boat – at the finish line, all the emotion comes out in a rush, and Holly and Jess agree to talk things over. It makes a difference to the prospects of the project, too: suddenly, there seems to be less pressure, less vulnerability. If they decide they want to change something in training, they've got the benefit of a good result behind them, and it'll be that little bit easier. They can be confident that they'll be in Poznań together for the next world cup in a couple of weeks, at Lucerne for the final one of the season in July, at the World Championships in Florida in September. And they're getting a bit of respect from the other members of the squad, not least because out of the four medals that the GB team brought back from Račice, the men were responsible for slightly fewer than one of them, and there's nothing wrong with a little bit of friendly inter-squad rivalry.

Meanwhile, Katherine Grainger has come down to see the quad in training, and has given them a few suggestions. She's gone through a few starts with them, and seems to be genuinely excited about their progress. And with Račice behind them, the bar has to be set high. The target now has to be to keep making finals, firstly at world cups and then at world championships, and to start pushing for medals. That would be a good year, not least because it would let the other countries know that the GB women's quad is back in business.

What could get in the way? A loss of form, of course, but

then that's what all the training's about. The return of a couple of crews who haven't competed internationally since Rio, per-haps – the Australians, the Chinese, the Americans. More ten-sions within the team, sure, but they now know they can row through that sort of thing. Maybe illness, though, or injury.

That could throw things a bit.

*

A EUROPEAN TOUR

One day in late October 2016, when the birds were singing, the sun was shining, and life in general was looking pretty good, Hannah Dines received an email.

Six weeks earlier, the 23-year-old Glaswegian had become a Paralympian. An elite tricyclist, the youngest rider in the combined T1/T2 field[6], she'd finished fifth in both the 15km time trial and the 30km road race. Three years after seeing her first female trike racer, and two years after seeing her second, she'd come within less than a minute of the road race podium. Up ahead, Carol Cooke and Jill Walsh, double gold and silver medallists respectively, clocked in at a combined age of 108. If for Jess Leyden the pain of missing out on Rio feels like something that will burn every day until she boards the plane to Tokyo, for Hannah the experience of the 2016 Games should simply have demonstrated – to her and those around her – that a Paralympic medal next time round was well within reach.

Then, as the days and weeks passed, there'd been a bit of a comedown. Of course there had. She'd been throwing herself headlong at the Paralympics since being taken on by British Cycling in the winter of 2014 – "a ski jump to Rio", her coach had called it – and suddenly to have that behind her took some adjustment. So instead of putting her feet up for a month, as British Cycling would normally recommend to their riders

6. The T1 and T2 classifications within para-cycling cover trike riders whose balance and coordination are impaired – with T1 being for those on whom the impact is more severe – and in a combined field, such as that at the Paralympics, finishing times for the time trial (but not the road race) will be factored accordingly. Hannah's a T2, although the classification criteria are a bit fuzzy – to the extent that the difference between the two might come down to a classifier's subjective assessment of the level of spasticity in one limb. This will, in due course, become highly relevant.

after such a big event, she joined team mate Karen Darke, rock climber turned adventurer turned Rio hand bike time trial gold medallist, on a camping holiday that turned into a cycling holiday in the Hebrides, and followed that up with the three days of punishing climbs and swooping turns that constituted the nascent Majorca Hand Bike Tour.

And then, a few days after she'd made it back into the country, she received an email.

Her results over the previous couple of years hadn't been good enough. Neither – and this was the sender's more immediate concern – had her power output. So she now, said British Cycling, had three months to find a ten per cent improvement on the power mark she had hit at Rio – which was already a personal best – and she would then have to be able to sustain that higher level for twenty minutes.

Hannah already knew a bit about power. John Hampshire, an independent coach who looked after Karen Darke, had been helping her on and off for a few months pre-Paralympics, and he'd loved going through the numbers from training and races. But Tom Hodgkinson, her coach at British Cycling, had never shown much apparent interest in it. He'd brought a lot of positive stuff to the table, certainly, but as far as Hannah was aware, he just didn't look at her performance in those sort of terms.

Still, there it was. And if that had been it, it might have been manageable. A racer's year, be they on bike or trike, in a boat or in spikes, is usually divided into winter training and summer competition, and the type of work that each involves is markedly different. In winter, it's endurance, volume, stamina; then for the races, it's fast twitch, short and sharp. Dedicating three months to a power target meant ditching the former for the latter, which would hurt her in the summer, but then if it kept her on programme, it would probably be worth it.

Except that wasn't all. If she hit this new power target,

British Cycling continued, she would then have another three months in which to go a further ten per cent better. Quite aside from wiping out an entire winter's worth of endurance training, that sounded pretty unlikely; and when, a while later, she discovered that the target that it all added up to was beyond the physical capabilities of both Carol Cooke and Jill Walsh, Hannah started to wonder.

At school, she hadn't been athletic. Reduced motor output, poor balance, high muscle tone, malformation of leg and foot soft tissues, all effects of neonatal cerebral palsy that had irrevocably shut down parts of her brain, meant being picked last, protected and patronised. She'd gone to university, planning for a future in medical research, and then, in the summer after her first year, she'd opened a magazine and seen a picture of a young boy running. It seemed impossible, but it looked brilliant, and so she'd got herself the thing the boy was using for support – something called a RaceRunner, with three wheels and a saddle but no pedals – and off she went. Within a year, she'd competed nationally and internationally at 100 metres, at 200 metres, at 400 metres, at 800 metres and at 1500.

She broke the world records in the lot of them.

So she came to the attention of British Cycling, who invited her along to a talent identification day. They put her on a trike, she ticked all the boxes, she made all the cut-offs, and so they put her into their development squad and started to point her towards Rio.

For all her promise, however, it became clear pretty quickly that her chances of a medal were slim at best. She was good, no question about it, ranking fourth in the world in the T2 class by the time 2016 came around. But gold and silver were out of the question – Carol and Jill were going to have those sewn up

– and bronze was going to be a stretch, because she'd almost certainly have to find a way past Jana Majunke, a German with four extra years of experience on her, and who had beaten her every time they'd raced.

When it came to selection time, they dressed it up as best they could, Hannah and her coach, and they said that she was aiming for a medal in the road race, even though there was next to no chance that was going to happen. And so she went to Rio – in part, to be honest, because her place had been ring-fenced by the UCI[7], in order to ensure that the trike races had enough entrants – and sure enough, she missed the podium.

The email wasn't done. In addition to the power targets, and a stipulation that she carry out a weekly training session dedicated to cornering – not in itself unreasonable, given that she has an additional balance disorder, not always part and parcel of cerebral palsy, which means she doesn't know where her limbs are in space – it said that Hannah needed to 'research and design a coping strategy for pre-race day nerves, with particular emphasis on the month leading into major selection or medal events'. She would then have to present this to the coaches at the same time as her first power test, and act on it throughout the racing season – assuming, that is, that they kept her on.

That felt like a bit of a puzzler too. Sure, there'd been a contretemps or two in the run-up to Rio. At the Ostend World Cup in May 2016, for instance, she'd bought a new chainset for the time trial. The standard policy at British Cycling at the time, as Hannah understood it, was that they would provide all bikes and deal with any mechanical needs, but for whatever reason that didn't seem to apply to the trike programme, so

7. The Union Cycliste Internationale, the world governing body for cycling.

Hannah bought herself a chainset. But then the mechanics who fitted it – and who would normally be expected to know all about what their riders were riding – either didn't notice or didn't tell Hannah that the cranks were too long. So Hannah spent the whole competition feeling unstable, aware that something was wrong but not knowing what and not being able to fix it, and getting herself into a fair bit of trouble with Tom and the management when she tried. She'd been anxious then all right, but it wasn't the sort of anxiety that a presentation can fix.

Yet be all that as it may, if you want to be the best, British Cycling is where you want to be, and so Hannah shelved some of her winter programme. Out went the long rides. In came indoor sprint sessions on the rollers, working up levels of power that she normally wouldn't approach until pre-race tuning. Through seven days a week of training, Christmas came and went, and all of a sudden it was 20th January and the first power test, and she missed the target by seven watts. Five days later, she was named in the British Cycling squad for the 2017 season, as published on its official website. A few days after that, they told her that that was a mistake, and she was out.

The presentation went well, though.

"I'm a bit scared of this," Hannah says. "It seems like lots of people – and British Cycling specifically – have this idea of the recipe for a gold medal athlete: that they are 100% committed to what they do, and they don't do anything else. Every decision they make, it's sport first, and other things second. I'm not like that. And I still think I can win a gold medal."

It's March 2017. She's now officially off the British Cycling programme, although her funding won't actually cut out for another month or so.[8] She can still race as an independent at this season's world cups – as with rowing, cycling has three world cup races a year, as well as an annual world championships – but she's going to need to find about £3,500 in running costs just to get through the season. Not only that, she's also had to sort out a new racing trike.

There hadn't been much wrong with the one she'd ridden in Rio. Designed by Nissan especially for the Paralympics, it had enjoyed a quiet Scottish Christmas in the back of Hannah's modified Honda Jazz while she was out in California visiting her cousins – spending the money, as it goes, that Nissan had been paying her to ride it. And then on New Year's Eve, while Hannah was still away, the car was stolen and joyridden into a petrol station, whereupon it went up, trike included, in a fireball. A new trike looked like costing around £7,500, and Hannah didn't have £7,500, so some of her friends suggested crowdfunding.

Within two days of setting up her appeal for donations, 350-plus people – Jill Walsh among them – had blown the target away. Dame Sarah Storey, Britain's greatest ever female Paralympian, gave some money too, and then went several steps further.

Hannah had been a member of the Boot Out Breast Cancer Cycling Club – a sister club to the elite women-only road Storey Racing team set up by Sarah and her husband Barney – while on the British Cycling programme, so Sarah knew a bit about her, and if for Hannah the invitation to join Storey Racing came out of the blue, for Sarah, it was an opportunity that she had been waiting for.

"I'd long been wanting to engage with another para-cyclist

---

8. Not that it was ever huge. Just before Rio, Hannah was on the 'academy' squad, and on the higher of its two levels of funding. That meant that they saw her as a future Paralympic medal prospect. It also meant that she was earning less than £800 per month.

in the teams I ran, but there was never the right person," she says. "Everyone of an equivalent standard to the non-disabled riders was already looked after within the GB team. Hannah was the first female rider to come off British Cycling who I felt still had her best years ahead of her, so I thought it was the right thing for our team to do to offer her a place."

That gave the season ahead a whole new complexion. It won't solve all her money worries, but she'll wear the Storey Racing colours at her races, and they'll pay towards her travel and racing costs, as well as medical support if necessary. On top of which, she's picked up support from the sportscotland institute of sport,[9] which doesn't actually have a funded programme for physically disabled road athletes, but is offering Hannah access to physiotherapy, strength and conditioning coaching, and nutritional advice; and finally, she's getting a bit of money from Winning Students, a national sports scholarship programme run in partnership with the Scottish Institute[10] and the Scottish Funding Council, to which she is getting access because she's taking an Open University course in creative writing. All of which means she can get through the next few months, which will do for now. The future can wait.

In the meantime, racing season is a couple of lowland world cups, in Belgium's Ostend and Emmen in Holland. Sandwiched in between those is a trip to the Cologne Classic, a three-day festival of cycling which will also feature, if the combination of its official website and Google Translate is to be believed, the enticing prospect of 'sorcery for children' in the

---

9. The high performance arm of Scotland's national sports agency, and yes, that's its official name. From now on, though, it's going to be referred to as the Scottish Institute, because names that are in all lower case are silly.
10. See, doesn't that look better?

main square. There should have been another world cup before any of these, in Maniago in the north-eastern Italian foothills, but having spent a winter working on sprinting rather than stamina and picking up an injury to boot, Hannah isn't quite ready for that.[11]

At first, it looks like this will cost her a chance of fighting her way back onto the British Cycling squad. Under the criteria that applied to her old funding arrangement, a medal or two in these world cups, maybe even some fourth places, and she might have been able to make it back in before the end of the year. But by the time Ostend comes around, she's learnt that changes are coming. From October, when the new rules will take effect, she will have to be within seven per cent of the gold medal-winning time at two world cup time trials within the same year. She rides at Ostend, and finishes in a solid enough fifth place again (on top of a fourth-place finish in the road race), but despite upping her power since Rio she's 12 per cent off Carol Cooke's winning time, with only one more world cup to go.

All of which means that Hannah will end up being presented with three different targets – and with power output giving way to placings, and then that in turn to time percentage, three different types of target – in less than a year. For all the turmoil that's surrounding British Cycling in the aftermath of Rio – the allegations of bullying, discrimination and favouritism involving Shane Sutton, Jess Varnish, Wendy Houvenaghel and indeed anyone, it seems, between whose mouth and han-

---

11. An aside. The results from the Maniago World Cup – and indeed any major para-cycling competition – are published pretty quickly on the UCI website. But they're not immediately obvious – you need to know exactly which parts of the website to look at, and at the time Maniago came around, Hannah didn't. In the aftermath of the races, therefore, she was texting her competitors to ask how things had gone. You don't hear much of Usain Bolt doing that.

dlebars there is room for a microphone – that seems an undue amount of uncertainty to unload onto an up-and-comer who has gone from the brink of a Paralympic medal to a struggle to stay in the sport.

But she's going to have to make the best of what she's got, and for one thing, she's managed to tag along for a few months with Carol Cooke. It started when Hannah told Carol about British Cycling dropping her, whereupon Carol got more and more outraged at what she saw as a missed opportunity to develop trike racing and said to Hannah, look, I'm going to be at the world cups and travelling around Europe on my own, why don't you join me? And when the world's best female trike racer makes an offer like that, you don't say no. So Hannah's paying towards fuel and food, and she'll be picking up advice from and training alongside Carol along the way. After Belgium it'll be Germany, where they'll be staying with Hans-Peter Durst, himself a double trike gold medallist at Rio; and then Carol should be able to get her access to the Australian training centre in Gavirate, in the Italian province of Varese – as coincidence would have it, by the very lake on which Jess has been training.

There are going to be limits to what Hannah can get out of all of this, though. For one, if there's a debate to be had about whether able-bodied athletes compete on a level playing field, there's simply no question when it comes to para-sport. Hannah has come to the trike from a background of lifelong cerebral palsy: she couldn't walk until her teens, and her legs have had to endure an awful lot of surgery. Both Carol and Jill Walsh, on the other hand, were talented amateur athletes and long-serving police officers – Carol in Toronto, Jill as a New York state trooper – before being diagnosed with multiple sclerosis in their mid-thirties and mid-forties respectively. So while their motor function is deteriorating and will continue to do so, they have the sorts of muscles that a 23-year-old student who's grown up with CP quite simply doesn't. On top of which, as Hannah puts it: "With cerebral palsy, you're very much falling asleep all the time. I get lots of fatigue, lots of dizziness, because after a big session my brain will just shut down."[12]

But if the advice of a 55-year-old with MS might not always be on point for someone with cerebral palsy who is less than half her age, and Carol's significantly quicker race pace means that they can't work together in the world cups without someone raising at least an eyebrow and more likely a formal complaint, what they can do is work on technique and technology; and so for starters, they're going to try out some aero bars[13] that Hannah's borrowed from Hans-Peter. Hannah hasn't used aero bars before, at least not at race level: basically, her left arm struggles with the position, and when she puts her hips and joints under pressure in ways they're not used to, it makes her

12. That also means that Hannah is limited in the amount of training she can do. Even over the winter, it might only be 11 hours or so of cycling per week, plus three hours in the gym and a few more hours of running around after teenagers as part of some volunteering work she's doing at Red Star, a Glasgow-based club for athletes with disabilities – about which more anon. For the moment at least, her body just won't let her do more. In the winter before Rio, she'd tried to add in another hour of cycling each week, to build herself up into a 20-hour-a-week, remorseless, relentless machine. The effort was great for her cardiovascular fitness. It also injured her hip.

13. You may be aware of the struggles of which Bertie Wooster spoke while telling his Jeeves stories – in short, as to how much background to bung in to ensure that the more familiar reader wasn't bored and the newcomer wasn't fogged. So too has it been a bit of a head-scratcher to work out which technical words need further explanation, and those for which, in the interests of a smoother narrative flow, it would be better to leave you to Google. Aero bars felt like one that would reward a bit more detail, so here goes – while they will be old friends to the semi-serious amateur cyclist and above, for anyone else, they're handlebars that point forward, allowing the rider to hunch down over her bike and tuck her arms in. Thus less drag, and more speed. Tally ho!

pedal stroke wonky, and she loses power. But Carol's going to talk her through how much she can do with the aero bars on, how much she can push through the times where she feels unstable but won't actually fall over, and then she can practise, and practise, and practise. In the meantime it's onwards, across the Channel and out into the continent.

Allons-y.

*

"DOES THIS HURT?"

First it was Mathilda, competing at Belgrade with her second rib injury in the space of four months. Then it was Holly's turn, with a rib problem of her own which briefly took her out of the boat completely. After Račice, Holly again, this time a bladder infection that fought off three different courses of antibiotics before finally succumbing to surgery; and then while she was still out of action, Beth came down with the norovirus.

Scratching the whole crew from the Poznań World Cup almost comes as a relief, before finally – is it finally? Surely it's finally, at least for this season – just as the four of them have made it back into the boat together in early June, Jess's rib goes too. So coach Thompson decides that they really can't race at the Henley Royal Regatta at the end of June either, and Jess heads down to see Liz Arnold, the team physio.

Liz pokes around for a bit. "Does this hurt?" she asks. "Nope," lies Jess, biting her lip. Ok, this is fine, I can ride this out. Maybe we can do Henley after all, that'd be sweet, especially after last year, that was fun. Racing, winning, chilling, drinking. Mathilda getting half-dragged and half-thrown through the open window of Wetherspoons – with the best of intentions, to be sure – and turning up at training the next day with a couple of layers of skin missing all the way from her knee down to her ankle.

Liz picks another area to prod. "Does that hurt?" Ah, now this is different. It does, yes, very much so, and you know what, Liz can probably tell, too, what with the screaming. "Roll over," she says. "No," replies Jess. "Er... ok. Sit up?" "No." And that's that. The quad will be going to Lucerne for the third and final race of the world cup series, but it's going to be with Alice Baatz, who finished seventh at trials, and not Jess.

Not that she's hugely fazed. "Before April, I'd have been worried," she says. "But I think at the moment, I just want the quad to go as fast as it can. I have no doubt in my mind that I would love them to get a medal at Lucerne, because I know that I'll be back in it – and if I'm not, I'll at least get a seat race." There are good reasons for Jess's sense of security – the boat's already won one "proper" medal with her in it, and she herself has the second-place finish at trials to fall back on – but it's not an outlook that's entirely shared throughout the crew.

"It's definitely part of the battle in your head," admits Holly. "How often depends on the person, but I think it will at least cross everyone's mind once, like: 'Oh crap, does that feel really good without me in it?'" The other three are a bit more self-confident, and that's slowly rubbing off on Holly, but there's always going to be a voice in her head: "I'm terrible. I'm not going to make it go faster."

For the while, though, none of them are in the boat, which means a bit of enforced downtime around Henley, and an opportunity, perhaps, to live a little. "Yes, we're full time athletes," Jess says, "but I didn't go to university. I'm still young, and I still want to go out every now and again." Holly adds that they've talked about putting in extra effort to do more outside rowing, to which Jess pipes up that she's recently been to see Little Mix. Mathilda, it transpires in the ensuing discussion, is not a huge fan of the chirpy foursome – which just goes to show that there's no accounting for taste.

So what else to do with their spare time? They could do a bit of extra-curricular training, of course, and some on the squad do just that. Jess's current housemate, for one, is the sort of person who will go home after a day at Caversham and watch rowing videos on YouTube. Which is, of course, absolutely fine if it works for you, but as far as these four are concerned, it'd make them feel like they were "on" 24/7, and it wouldn't be healthy. I need to get home at this time. I need to recover, I need to prepare my meals, I need to go to bed, I need to get up, I need to do it all again.

What about an extra session here and there? Surely that couldn't hurt? Nope, they say, you've got to trust the coaching staff. "Day to day, you'd have time to go and do another session," says Jess, "but then you're just stuffing yourself over for the next one. And you get really told off if you're ever found out. People have done it, and the head coaches have just been like, 'Well, why am I here? Why are you bothering listening to me, if you're not doing what I say?'" Mathilda chips in: "I did that before Christmas, actually, trying to fit in four sessions a day on top of my degree,[14] but it wasn't worth it. I made myself ill for six weeks, and British Rowing went mental."

So it's a drink or two here, a coffee and cake there, catching up with friends and family, nothing too dramatic.

And then off they go to Lucerne, Mathilda and Beth and Holly and Alice, leaving Jess back at home, working through her rehab. To start with, it's going fine – the rib clears up within a couple of weeks. But then the days roll by and something is still hurting, in fact it's getting worse and worse, and somehow no-one seems to know what the problem is or how to treat it. The pain has worked its way down to the hip, and five weeks becomes six becomes seven, and suddenly Jess can't see an end-point, and she's struggling.

Meanwhile, the racing has brought mixed news for the patched-up GB crew. With a new order in the boat – Mathilda

---

14. She's studying chemistry part time at Reading University, so will be juggling rowing and coursework until at least 2019.

at stroke, and Holly, Alice and Beth behind her – they finish third in the heats and a hard-earned second in the repêchage, but they can't make any impression in the final, and can only scrap their way to fifth. Ahead, Poland – who've managed to keep the same crew together all year – round off a perfect world cup season with their third gold, with the Netherlands, Australia and Germany puffing in behind them.

At least rehab is keeping Jess busy. There's swimming, and then cross-training, and physiotherapy, and soft tissue appointments, and all in all it seems to take up more time than normal training ever does. And then, finally, the medical staff find the tears in her hip. They tell her that her hip flexors have been hanging on, tightening up and not letting go – which is good to hear in a way, because it ties in with something that's been afflicting a few people in the team. A few of the men's squad have had hip operations to remove extraneous bits of bone, and Jess's MRI scan has shown the start of something similar.

It's a common problem among rowers, she learns, with its root cause in the fact that from a young age, they're putting unusually large loads into their hips under extreme flexion. That, over time, leads to bone spurs, which in turn leads to tears in the joint, which is moving more because of the bone; and all of that leads to inflammation, which is the bit that hurts. Jess's has been picked up relatively early, so she should be able to manage it without the need for surgery, but there'll be particular pre-training exercises she'll have to do for the foreseeable future, switching the right muscles on and the wrong ones off, and she'll have to work a lot on strengthening in the gym.

That should all be doable, though; and psychologically, she's just about got by. She's been frustrated, certainly, but she's been happy enough within herself, and she's been getting out and about rather than holing herself up with her thoughts. Could she, perhaps, save up the real darkest hour stuff, the crying alone in her room with all hope gone, until, say, the February of Olympic year, before an improbable, last-gasp rise to glory in Tokyo?

And she laughs – sort of – and says no, let's not do that.

*

COULDN'T BE HAPPIER

The car's packed, but Hannah couldn't tell you how.

It's got two trikes in it, and that alone would test the very best of us. Both riders have a set of race wheels too, so that's six extra wheels, not to mention the spare parts they might need if something goes wrong or falls off. Then there's two big bags of luggage. Hannah's brought a mattress topper as well, just in case she gets to a competition and the place she's staying doesn't have the best bed; and finally, there needs to be room for her pillow and for the little bag of contingencies – proper ketchup, oats for your porridge, stuff like that. By some form of witchcraft, the whole lot fits in to the Citroën Berlingo in which the Briton and the Aussie will be tooling around Europe, and Carol Cooke, who evidently spent much of the 1980s and 1990s parked in front of Tetris, is standing next to it all looking pretty damn chuffed.

After Ostend, they hit the road for a four-hour trip through three countries over to Dortmund, and two weeks in the company of Hans-Peter Durst and his wife Ulrike. There are parties – every day, it seems like, and it's Hans-Peter's birthday just before racing starts at the Cologne Classic too, so that kicks things up a notch. The wine flows, and Hannah looks on forlornly because she doesn't drink in race season, and off she goes for a nap and back she comes and they're still going strong.

Then from time to time, where they can fit it in among all the revelry, they go out training. Hans-Peter's building up for a 134km stage race in the mountains, so he's out of Carol and Hannah's league in a physical sense, but they can all stick together for a bit. Sometimes, Hans-Peter and Carol just watch Hannah doing shuttles in the little alleyway by Hans-Peter's house, and on one of those runs, they realise that for a few years now, she's been cornering all wrong.

It takes a while to get to grips with exactly what she needs to change, though, and then it's even harder for her to put their advice into practice. "I make gains when I train," she explains. "But as soon as the adrenaline kicks in during the race, it's like my body isn't mine any more. On the straight, I can push my legs – or at least the muscles I can control – and I can make them burn as hard as I want. And I enjoy that, because that's the feedback mechanism. That tells me that I'm working. But with cornering, my brain is almost paralysed. I get so much worse."

There are logistical difficulties too. Hannah needs to practise on roads. On most roads, though, she can't practise cornering at any sort of speed, because most roads have cars on them. Hans-Peter and Carol's reflexes are that bit quicker, so they can come into a corner, check it's safe to go, and then go. "But that's way too much information for me," Hannah says. "I have to slow down and stop."

Then there's the handlebars. Hannah's still struggling to work with the aero bars that she wants to use for her time trialling. They're great for aerodynamics, but the position they put her in on the trike puts pressure on her hips. A fully able-bodied rider normally spreads their pedalling effort between quads, calves, hip flexors and glutes, but Hannah's disability means that she can't use her calves, and the quads actually take away from the power that her hip flexors can produce. To sum it all up – if she uses the aero bars, she'll be sacrificing some of her power, albeit that, in exchange, she'll be able to reduce her air resistance and cut down on the wobbling.[15]

She's also talked to Carol and Hans-Peter about handlebars for the road races. Most elite riders, on trikes or two wheelers,

15. It's a balancing act.

will use a racing handlebar – the curved one, that looks a bit like a ram's horns. When Hannah was first taken on by British Cycling, that's what they gave her, and so that's what she's been riding with. But some people on the para circuit, generally those with poor hand control, use mountain bike handlebars instead, that just go straight out sideways. A couple of the trike pack use them, and Carol thinks that they'd be good for Hannah too, because at the moment her arm position isn't helping with the cornering. But – and this is becoming a familiar problem – making a change is going to cost a lot of money; and it's not just a question of buying a new handlebar set: she's also going to have to re-tune the gears. So it's going to take time, too. She'll contact some bike shops, and ask really, really nicely, and if something comes of it, she'll trial things out on her training trike over the winter, and see what happens.

First, Cologne. It's a mixed-gender race where the men's times are adjusted to give one overall ranking, and Hannah comes fourth. She's third among the women, which is pretty much what she was expecting given the absences of Jill Walsh and of Monica Sereda, the latter of whom is new to the circuit since Rio but managed to sneak ahead of Hannah at the Ostend time trial. Between her and Carol on the women's podium is Jana Majunke, and Hannah reckons that she'd be pushing Jana seriously close if only she'd enjoyed a proper winter's training.

But the racing's great. It's basically a big integrated multi-sport festival, with international para and able-bodied riders mixing with less mainstream sports – your cross-country roller-skating and the like – and the crowds are heaving. The closed roads and the number of spectators this attracts helps with the atmosphere, and riding on a course which is pretty much entirely made up of right hand turns helps with Hannah's performance.

It's unusual for a course to be right hand heavy, but when they are, it's to her advantage. The right side of her body is less affected by her cerebral palsy, and while she hasn't asked all of her competitors which side they favour, Carol seems to be pretty left side dominant, and so does Jana, and so does Jill. For all that, though, she suspects that there won't be many corners at all come Tokyo, if only because the organisers aren't going to want everyone to take them on too fast and come crumpling down in a heap on the tarmac.

Onwards, ever onwards, and June sees Carol and Hannah at the Australian training centre in Italy, where they rub shoulders with some of the Australian able-bodied rowing squad and Hannah meets a man called Monty Summers.

Monty's in his late 20s. He was a cross-country runner in his youth, and good enough at it to make it to national championships level in the mid-2000s. Then, he was diagnosed with acute lymphoblastic leukaemia. He reacted badly to the bone marrow transplant – for days on end, he was on a morphine drip and being fed through a tube – but slowly, he got better, and bit by bit, he got fitter.

Within three years, he had returned to athletics, and within seven, he was representing his country. He's never going to be an Olympian – he's not quick enough – and he's not going to be a Paralympian either, because he's not disabled enough. So he combines his full time job – helping people with disabilities into sport – with trips to the gym and sessions on the track, and every couple of years, he does the only thing he's ever really wanted to do – he runs – and he wins medal after medal after medal for Australia at the World Transplant Games. So, you know, don't let it stop you, whatever it is.

From Italy to Emmen, and Hannah's second and final world cup of the year. The time trial comes and goes, and it's another fourth place. Carol wins, of course she does, Jill comes second, Jana picks up the bronze, and Hannah's never really in contention. But somehow, at the road race the following day, something's different. She's dropped every lap, at the same damn corner each time, and every lap she sprints back up to the leaders.

Normally, that would cost her. Come the business end of the race, she'd have nothing left, she wouldn't be able to keep up with Carol or Jill or Jana, and she'd drift back to her usual place among the also-rans. This time, though, the finishing line gets closer and closer, and hang on a moment, they haven't managed to shift her and she realises that she's going to get bronze. Carol and Jill are too far ahead, gold and silver have gone, but she's holding off Jana, who's in her slipstream but just can't find a way past. It's a real effort for Hannah to keep blocking her off, because she has to keep on reacting as Jana tries to flick round her, and the strain is making her wobble like crazy, but she's holding it, and holding it, and the two of them reach a corner, and Jana's coach is there and he knows it's gone and he's screaming at his rider. "What's happened? What's happened? You've ruined it! You've ruined it!"

And maybe that distracts Hannah, who lets herself think for just a fraction of a second that Jana's given up, she won't try it here, she'll wait until after the corner, and suddenly bam! Jana's round her and gone. And Hannah could outsprint her if only they were just a bit closer to the finish, but she's let her go from too far out, and Jana's too far ahead, and sure enough, while Hannah may have finished less than half a minute back from gold,[16] it's another race where she's watching three other people pick up the medals and the flowers from the pretty ladies with their high heels and their interchangeable faces and their dresses made from a quantity of material that might just about stretch to a serviceable hand towel.

And she couldn't be happier.

The season-ending World Championships goes to form. Carol wins the women's races, Hans-Peter wins the men's. Behind Carol, the usual suspects – but no Hannah.[17]

Maybe she could have been out in Pietermaritzburg, if only she could have just held off Jana in Emmen. You can ask British Cycling to take you even if you're off the programme, and while the official criterion was a world cup gold, maybe she could have made the case that she was a good podium prospect, and that that's not to be sniffed at. But without that medal, there doesn't seem much point. Why are you even trying? they'd say. You're clearly not good enough.

"I don't want them to think of me in a negative light in terms of performance," Hannah says. "I'd rather give in the application form when there's something positive to put on it." She does end up wondering – given that nine GB riders went to South Africa, and they certainly didn't all win gold this season – whether it might have been worth putting in an application after all; but there it is.

"The summer that I've had, it's been incredible," she says.

16. By way of comparison, at Ostend, she'd been nine minutes back from Carol. That doesn't tell the full story, of course – Ostend was about tactics, and holding off Monica Sereda for fourth, because if they'd caught up to the front three, Monica might have been able to work with them and leave Hannah behind – but it's a definite improvement.

17. You could watch most of it streamed live on the UCI website, which is great. On the other hand, there was no commentary, no sound whatsoever in fact on the time trial, and of the fewer than 300 people that were watching the stream, one of them was me, and one of them was Hannah, which doesn't feel much like outreach.

"It's had no stresses and no bad points in it, I've had no episodes of howling or having angst. I've been absolutely, totally contented with life, and I've really enjoyed the plan that unfolded.

"I'm really not stressing about not being in the top three now. It's a long, long road, a very gradual thing, and I need to put in a lot. I won't be able to see it myself, and I'm sure I'll go through several mini-breakdowns, thinking that I've not got anywhere. And actually, that's good. Getting golds now would be such a big leap, it would probably signify that something was wrong. Doing it more gradually, that's more healthy."

What's made the difference, then? "I stayed out in Europe and trained," she reckons. "I still train at home, obviously, but there's nothing like Italian roads, or just being out of your home environment, with all your responsibilities. And also, just being with other trikes. In Scotland, I'm the only one, so I'm always riding with people on two-wheelers. And that can be quite discouraging, because they're always slowing down, and helping me out, whereas with Carol, for instance, it's not like she's doing it for me. She's going to do her training anyway, and she does it at her pace, and I'm there, and that's my pace too."

Of course, Carol has more than enough pace in South Africa to win yet another double gold, and so she takes her usual spot on the top step of a podium that is, frankly, looking a bit scuffed – lick of paint, fellas, come on now, it's a world championships. Ah, but look here, it's not Jill with the road race silver, it's Jana. Well, well. Sure, Jill had a crash this time, but that's not totally unheard of, and she'd usually get back on and be able to power her way back into silver anyway – a bit like back in Emmen, when Carol sprinted to gold on a flat tyre. But it does show how things could have played out for Hannah too, and if she can get in a good winter of endurance training this time around, maybe she can be right up there come spring.

The winter starts with a few club-level time trials, dotted around Scotland and the north of England. Racing a trike means that it's hard not to come last, but it's easy to pick up a lot of support if you're one of the few youngsters, one of the even fewer women, and quite literally the only person on three wheels rather than two. It stands to reason, what's more, that if you're the only trike, you're the fastest trike, so occasionally, Hannah even wins some cash.

She takes on the National Championships, a ten miler around Cockermouth, in early September, and then it's time for a break from the racing. She's been accepted onto a part-time Master's degree in Sport and Exercise Physiology at Manchester Metropolitan University, and after a painstaking trawl of potential living arrangements, she tracks down a spare room in a grade II listed place called Gatley Hall, which is in the Manchester suburb that shares its name, a bit ramshackle, quite popular with the local spider population, and notwithstanding all of the above, definitely neither haunted nor owned by a mysterious recluse with a shed full of sharp tools and a fondness for the night.

It's convenient for catching up with old friends and former and (hopefully) future team mates, and while Gatley itself isn't super quiet, getting out into the countryside for an undisturbed training ride takes half the time that it did when Hannah was based in Glasgow. So, for the next six months at least, it's going to be home. She's been given a sports scholarship by the university, which will give her access to support services – soft tissue massage, nutrition, performance and lifestyle, that sort of thing – so she shouldn't miss out on too much that she'd have had north of the border. Meanwhile, John Hampshire, who has been working as Hannah's full time coach ever since she got kicked off British Cycling, is a nomadic sort who arranges training diaries, puts together power graphs and gives advice over Skype from his camper van that's currently somewhere unspecified out in mainland Europe. And if that sounds a bit unorthodox, then as long as it keeps working for him, it means Hannah's not going to miss out on his input as a result of her move either.

She's still with Storey Racing, which is particularly good news given that if you asked her right now she'd describe Sarah as the most supportive and helpful manager she's ever had, and the Scottish Institute have promised not to forget about her. On the side, meanwhile, she's getting the occasional paid article into Scottish national broadsheet the *Herald*, on issues ranging from the classification system in para-sport to the rather odd approach that she received from the producers of Channel 4 programme *The Undateables* asking her to help them recruit people with disabilities to appear on the show. When she looks into it, the programme seems to have honest intentions, but to her mind, they're lost behind the title. "I have many qualities that make me undateable", she writes. "None of them are to do with my disability."

But leaving that aside, and ignoring the fact that she's been effectively airbrushed out of British Cycling for the time being – if you just went off their website and Twitter feed, you wouldn't know she was still in the sport – she's happy with how things are looking right now. She reckons she's going to pick up a world cup bronze medal or two next year, and she's allowing herself a glance towards Tokyo.

"Obviously, I don't know what I'll be like then," she says, "but I do believe that I can hurt myself more than Carol and Jill. It's going to be very close, there's going to be seconds in it, and I'm probably going to crash, have to get up with blood on my face, and I'll cross that finishing line with seconds to go because I'm able to go that extra tiny little bit. That's how I'm going to do it."

She'll have to fight her way back onto the British Cycling squad before then, but there's plenty of time for that. Maybe the squad selection criteria will change, or maybe her results will and they won't be able to ignore her. In the meantime, she's going to keep on keeping on.

Margaret Owen, Vicky Gunn, Griff Dines and Sally-Anne McDougall[18] didn't raise no quitter.

*

18. So Hannah's biological mum and dad are Margaret and Griff; they got divorced, and Griff got remarried with Sally-Anne and Margaret got remarried with Vicky; and yes, that's a lot of mothers.

THE WORLDS AND BACK AGAIN

It's been a funny old year. After a long time lying fallow, the Great Britain women's quad is coming into the 2017 World Championships with two bronze medals.

One of them, at the Europeans, was out of the blue and fantastic. The other, in Belgrade at the start of the season, was disappointing and entirely expected. There's been a no-show – the scratching from Poznań – and there's been the curate's egg of a fifth place with a patched-up, shifted-around crew at the Lucerne World Cup. There have been persistent injuries and odd illnesses. They've even managed to squeeze in Beth having her wisdom teeth out after a flare-up on the flight back from the squad's pre-world championships camp in Varese.

But for all that, the head-scratching won't be confined to the British. All in all, eleven nations have raced at the four main events so far, but five of those – France, Belarus, Romania, Russia and Ukraine – only turned up for the Europeans. Poland and the Netherlands have been the stand-outs, but while the Poles were imperious at the world cups, they finished behind Britain at Račice and missed out on the podium completely. The Netherlands have three silvers but no victory; Australia have been there or thereabouts without ever really getting themselves noticed; and China turned up at Poznań and came third before sending a boatful of teenagers to Lucerne and getting blown out of the water. And we haven't even seen the Americans, the defending world champions from two years ago, but who haven't raced at all this year, and who have come here without any of the four who took the boat to victory back in 2015.

At least the Varese camp saw Jess, Holly, Mathilda and Beth together in the same boat for a while, which hadn't happened for months. The rhythm seems to be improving, and that's coming through in the numbers too – they've been regularly towards the top of the pack on percentage gold medal time,[19] up in the nineties or thereabouts. So it's in high spirits that they pop back to Caversham for a week before flying out to Florida, which itself has emerged just about unbowed following a battering from Hurricane Irma.

Being back home feels strange. Varese was pretty full on, and so the overwhelming atmosphere around Caversham is rather like it normally is when the squad is returning from a competition – a bit flat, a bit tired. The mileage has been dialled down a little – just the 15k or so per day, that sort of thing, although it'll tick up again in the early part of the pre-racing week in Florida. Just before they go, on the Friday before the weekend they fly out, there will be intra-squad races, with similarly quick crews pitted against each other to try to get the competitive juices flowing and to iron out race plans. The quad will be racing the men's lightweight double, whose target time is only about a second quicker than their own, and who have the added benefit, as far as Jess and the others are concerned, of being men who'll be extra keen not to lose to girls. The start list for the regatta is out too, and everyone who's been a contender this season is going to be there, so it should give a pretty good idea of who's where and what's what.

If the original target was making the A final, then they cut their first crack seriously close. It's a strong start from Poland in the

19. For each boat class, the coaches at British Rowing set a time for which they can say to the crew: if you can hit this, you're likely to win Olympic gold. They're set a bit faster than world record pace, a couple of seconds maybe, and then "percentage gold medal time" measures how close you're getting – for the full race distance, and then scaled down through the rest of the training programme.

heat, and there's not much between Britain, Germany and the United States at 500 metres. But as the German challenge fades – was it the Europeans that was the anomaly for them this season? – it's the Americans who somewhat unexpectedly pull out into a halfway lead. Poland respond, and they're going to sail through, but the US are still well up on Great Britain at 1500, and it takes Mathilda calling for a furious final 500 metres to get them into a photo finish. And perhaps they would have been fine in the repêchage. Thankfully, however, by 1/100th of a second, they're not going to have to worry about that.

Automatic qualification leaves them with the best part of a week to fill, which comes at a time in her life when Jess is beginning to surprise herself with how much she enjoys her own company. Since she was 15, she's been going on rowing camps, letting others set the timetable, not really doing her own thing, and perhaps as a result, she's grown up thinking of herself as a very social person. But something's been building, through Varese, through the Caversham camp, through the couple of weeks in Florida before the racing started and during these few days when they're trying to keep fresh but also not let things slip, doing sessions but not actually racing, ticking over but itching to get going and then get out.

Jess keeps it under control, or at least she thinks she does, but she's relishing the little pockets of time on her own; so one morning, after Mathilda heads down to breakfast, Jess lingers behind in the room that they're sharing and just takes a moment to herself. It's nothing too dramatic, just a breath or two of calm, and then off she goes, down to breakfast and then onto one of the buses that will take everyone off to the morning's training.

Off the bus, over to the bag drop, and then out to the boat, and she's the first one there. And one, two, three people come up to her, and they're looking a bit perturbed. "Have you seen your crew?" "Er, no, I'm just waiting for them." "They're really worried about you." Ok, well, I've just had my breakfast and got on a bus, not quite sure what the issue is here.

Paul Thompson's next to arrive. "Oh, Jess, just make sure you're a bit earlier for the bus next time. You know, just to manage people's stress." Right ho, that's fine, I'll be there five minutes earlier, we hadn't talked about a time before this and it's not like I missed the bus or anything but whatever, I don't want to cause a problem for anyone.

And then Beth turns up and has a bit of a go at Jess for not being where she was supposed to be, and Jess takes umbrage because as far as she's concerned she wasn't *supposed* to be anywhere, and after they've finished the session and gone back to the hotel, there's enough resentment lingering that it's time for another clear-the-air chat between the four of them. And if by the end everyone's kissed and made up and it's all been about the stress really, it's still a bit of a waste of energy a couple of days before a world championships final.

At 500, they were gone. Poland – of course Poland – jump out almost from the first dip of blade into water. The Dutch, brave but outgunned again; Australia and Germany having a go from the outside lanes, and it's Britain against the United States for the honour of not coming last. You can't afford to let the field get away in the final of a world champs, but with 600 metres down Jess and the crew are already 12 metres back from the Poles, and if it's not quite getting worse, it's certainly not getting better. Out front, meanwhile, it's settling into a procession to the line. Poland have pulled out to seven, eight metres in front of the Dutch – a good half a boat length – and that gap is going absolutely nowhere as they reach halfway. They're in control.

One kilometre down, one to go, and maybe there's been a little something from Britain. Poland are still in command, and Jess and the crew aren't laying a glove on them, but the Australians and the Germans are sliding back into the pack; and suddenly, with 1150 gone, there are four boats fighting for bronze. 1250, 1300, and the US don't seem to be making any inroads, but there's now nothing, literally nothing, between Australia, Germany and Britain.

And Mathilda gives the call and they go, oars in and through and out and back, and while it's not perfect and seamless and smooth and effortless – it never is – a stroke rate of 35 becomes 36, and then 37. The other crews are winding it up too, and they're hitting higher stroke rates, but nobody's going faster than the British, and Poland are rocking. Katarzyna Zillmann looks cool enough in the stroke seat, but the pain is coursing through Maria Springwald and Marta Wieliczko behind her, and there's fear in the face of Agnieszka Kobus at bow.

The Netherlands haven't managed to close the gap as they come into the last 500, but they've hung on, and unlike the crew to which they've been losing all season long, they look smooth. And there's Great Britain! They've come through the Australians, they're pulling away from Germany, and with three hundred to go, they couldn't, could they? It's part of Beth's job to keep an eye on where they are in the field, and she's told the crew a couple of hundred back that they were in bronze; and while as far as Jess knows, that could be bollocks, she trusts Beth in what she's really saying, and that is: just fucking keep going, you lot, keep going, and you're going to win a world medal.

My god, what power! They're eating up the lake, metre by metre by metre, and they're doing it at the lowest stroke rate of anyone. Mathilda's chipped in again too – "We're in third, the Germans are attacking, we need to go," but she's undersold it, because the British are, right this second, the best, the smoothest, the strongest boat out on the water.

But then the Netherlands respond to this monster hunting them down from the lane inside, and they up the stroke rate to 40, 41, and Poland are shot, and within 100 metres the Dutch have gone from a third of a length back on the triple world cup winners to poking a bow ball ahead, and the line just a few more strokes away.

And if this race were 2,500m rather than 2k, you'd have had the Brits nailed on to row straight through both of them. But the finish line comes too soon, and it's the Netherlands who sink to their knees in the boat in exhaustion and disbelief, and broken Polish bodies that simply collapse in despair, and Jess and Holly and Mathilda and Beth will have to settle for bronze; but if Belgrade was depressing and Račice was a lonely light in the gloom, then this bronze medal is one to savour.

And then, once they've been through doping control and survived an interview with BBC TV in the course of which Holly slowly edges out of shot so she can have a quick lie down, Jess is gone, away from it all for just a little while. For a blissful week, she's on her own in Peru, the highlight of her trip the Lares trek, a loose rocks, no path, hands and knees scramble up and over the mountains. Then it's a week in Devon and Cornwall, a week back at home, and then, in the final week of October, back into training.

It doesn't start well. They're doing weights on the first day back, and Jess is happily chatting away to her weights coach while she's at it, when all of a sudden everything goes a bit wibbly and she realises she needs to sit down, right where she is and straight away. For a moment or two, her hearing's gone too; and as she tunes shakily back into her surroundings, it's

not to an outpouring of sympathy. "That's what a fat, seden-
tary person feels like all the time," says the coach with a smirk.

But after the first few days, it's not awful. There's a twenty
minute ergo session in which Jess comes top out of everyone,
and she's been out in the quad a few times and it's feeling pretty
good. Meanwhile, there's various physiological stuff going on,
and about three weeks in to the new season, everyone heads
down to London to undergo something called – for some reason – Flock of Birds. It's a full physio screening, pioneered
by Imperial College and run by Paul Thompson's wife, which
involves measuring the angles of your hips, your shoulders,
your ankles, your hamstrings, you name it. They put sensors
on your knees and your back and your spine, and they measure
the force you can put through a hooked-up ergo, and all sorts.
There was going to be a reward to all this, with Jess joining up
with Holly, Beth and Vicky Thornley to compete in the Fours
Head of the River, but at the last minute, Jess picks up a bout
of illness, and Kat Copeland has to stand in.

There's been too much illness and injury, if we're honest.
British Rowing have a metric called 'adherence to training',
which essentially summarises how well you stick to the pre-
scribed programme – if you're missing days through injury or
illness, even if you're there but just on a bike rather than out on
the water, you're going to get marked down. And if it seems a
little harsh to pull people up for this sort of thing, there are at
least steps that everyone can take. Jess is going to make a point
of going to bed by about 10ish this year, and she can make sure
that she keeps using hand sanitiser, and that she sticks to the
stretching programme that was put in place after her injury last
season, things like that.

Because fair or otherwise, adherence to training is something
that the coaches notice, and it's a measure by which Jess is near
enough the worst in the entire women's squad. She's not the

worst of the lot, that's Holly; but she's not doing as well as the third worst – and that's Beth. This is a quad which has got quite a bit of room for improvement.

If, that is, it stays as it is. No-one's seat is safe. This four could stay together for the next year and a half and qualify the boat for Tokyo at the 2019 World Championships – the first time of asking – and any and all of them could still be replaced in the final months before the Games if the coaches think that another combination might make it go faster. They all want to carry on though, which is a start, and it's hard to see Vicky Thornley wanting to give up her single, so even if final trials in April throw up another couple of contenders, then in the short term you'd have to think they'll be given the chance to do seat races at the very least.

The first assessment takes place during the first weekend in November, and as with last year's, it paints an incomplete picture. For returning Olympians who were exempt in 2016, read the returning World Championships crews this time around, so there's not much information to work with on who's going to be a threat to the top boats. Zoë Lee wins on her return from a year out with injury, but her background's in sweep; Georgina Brayshaw, who came ninth in final trials for 2017, is second; Jess's housemate Emily Carmichael is sixth and Mathilda's sister Charlotte is tenth. If there's anyone in particular to look out for, it might be Lucy Glover, an 18-year-old who won gold in the quad at the Under-23 World Championships back in July, and who comes in fourth – but it's a long time until April, so who knows.

For Jess, the aim at this stage is simply to get back into the quad. If that happens, then it's about consistently challenging for medals at the world cups and the Europeans. In the meantime, she'll also be trying to keep up with the Open University engineering course that she's just restarted, and which is currently going fine except that they've introduced a time limit for completing the course that wasn't there last year. It's not too onerous a deadline – she's got another five years after this one, although she does have the work she should have done last year to squeeze in on top of the regular modules. All in all, it adds up to about 20 hours per week, as well as a week's residential course that she'll have to do at some point during the 2018 season. But she's feeling a bit more organised, a bit more on top of things, so hopefully for a little while, everything can just tick over.

*

JOHN BOY

When she was three years old, Jess Leyden's dad brought home a little motorised quad bike, and her mum nearly had a fit. "She's too young, John! She can't—"; "Oh, stop worrying about it, Sharon," he'd said. "Let her have a good time."

And to be fair to him, she did. Within twenty-four hours, he'd fiddled with the mechanism and taken out the speed restrictor, and then off she went, tearing around the fields near their family home in the West Yorkshire town of Todmorden, not an ounce of fear.

As they tend to do when you're three, the quad bike phase passed; but only to give way to horses. Horses scared Sharon a bit too, but she decided that she'd have to grow to like them for the sake of her daughter, and so she'd do all the walking, miles and miles across the moors, and Jess would come home from school and say, "Can we go out, Mum?" Which meant three more hours over the hills, a vanishingly appealing prospect as the cold winter nights drew in. "Yeah, course we can, Jess."

That lasted a bit longer, five or six years of going out riding with John and joining the hunt until that got banned and they switched over to drag hunting instead – and that cheered Sharon right up, because being the vegetarian she was, the thought of her daughter coming home with blood on her face had made her stomach churn.

One day, when Jess was about twelve, she went out with her dad again and a friend's pony came along too, a frolicsome sort called Chester. John told Jess not to ride too close to Chester, because he knew that the horse kicked out hard when he went into canter; but Jess wanted to be up at the front, because that's where she usually was, and of course the horse kicked out and caught her flush on the elbow.

Down she went, and straight off to hospital, although they didn't tell Sharon straight away, because she was back home preparing the buffet for a big birthday party later that day and they didn't want her to worry and – more to the point – stop cooking. The evening came, and Sharon kept asking Peter, her eldest, "Where's our Jessica?" "Oh don't worry mum, she's coming in a minute." And so she was, with her arm in a sling, and of course Sharon flipped. "Why didn't you tell me?" "Well, you'd stop doing the buffet." All about priorities.

But the injury scuppered the horse riding for the time being, so what to do next?

Peter had recently gone off to Manchester University, and he hadn't been there long before he was calling his mum up to say that he wanted to join the Royal Air Force. Sharon, having been in the navy herself back in the day, thought that sounded like a good idea; but then Peter added that he needed to find a group activity to join in with as a part of his training.

It seemed a bit rich to be asking his mother for advice – he wanted to join the RAF, but he couldn't think of a group activity for himself, without asking his mum? – but there it was, he wanted to know what she thought. And because she had just been doing the ironing in front of some footage of Steve Redgrave winning one of his Olympic gold medals, she said, "What about rowing?" She didn't really think before she said it, she didn't know anything about the sport, didn't really care about it, was still a bit annoyed at Peter for not finding his own way, but the seed was sown, and Peter joined the university rowing club.

He was pretty good, in his way. They went to watch him race once, in Liverpool, which was fun. And in her turn, little, twelve-year-old Jess, who couldn't straighten her arm – she still can't, not fully – and couldn't, at least for the time being, get back on the horse, thought she might fancy giving rowing a try too. She'd found out that Todmorden High School had signed up for Project Oarsome, a campaign *launched by Redgrave and funded by Sport England with the aim of getting young people onto the water, and so she and about 15 other kids took the bus up to nearby Hollingworth Lake with PE teacher Gemma Cooper, and one by one the others dropped out until it was just Jess.*

And even then, it could have been a wipe-out. Jess had enjoyed coming down from school, and she'd started coming in her own time too, but there simply wasn't much going on for her at the club until a man called Ian John, who'd always coached adults and who'd never sculled in his life, decided to take her and a couple of other girls who were just sort of mooching around, and put them to the test.

Jess wasn't outstanding. She didn't stand out physically, never did and never has, but she was a nice kid, and Ian got on with Sharon as well, and you tend to look after people who are nice to you back, don't you? And she loved it. She loved coming to the club, she loved doing the training, even from the early days. Her first race, and she crashed into a bank, and she still loved it. And as time went on, and Ian picked up just enough sculling technique to keep himself useful on that side of things, he would change up her training schedule and she would take it on, without question.

She started winning at the northern regattas, at Tees and Chester and Northwich, and within two years, she'd improved enough for Ian to enter her for the 2009 National Championships, at Holme Pierrepont on the outskirts of Nottingham.

They thought she might do quite well, but in truth, no-one around Jess had had any real experience of elite rowing, so they didn't have much of an idea what to expect. Sharon couldn't bear to watch the race – she almost never has, she gets too nervous – and John didn't like coming either, he didn't want to get in the way; so Ian and his wife Denise set themselves up on the bank and Ian got out his video camera and Denise took up her binoculars.

Ian couldn't really see Jess through the wind and the rough water, so he tuned himself into the commentator, who was reporting over the tannoy about how a girl from Tees Rowing Club had started strongly, and was beginning to pull away from the field.

He ignored Denise elbowing him, because he was trying to video the race to go through it with Jess afterwards, but he couldn't pretend he wasn't a bit puzzled, because they'd thought she'd do all right, and there was simply no mention of her. And Denise kept on elbowing him ("No, no, he's got it wrong!"), and he kept on ignoring her, until halfway through the race the commentator handed over to someone else, whose job was to talk the crowd through the second kilometre, and who – unlike his colleague – had noticed the little blonde girl who was so far ahead of the rest that it looked like she was warming down from the previous race.

That changed things.

"Right," said Jess. "What are we going to enter next?"

And then one day, about a year or so after that, John went out with the hunt, on the back of his new horse. The two of them flashed through the countryside, wind rushing through their hair, John in his element. You couldn't keep him down, Sharon says. His glass was always half full, he was the centre of attention wherever he went, and Jess adored him.

Sharon's thought a lot since that day about a poem that she can't quite remember, but it talks about the feel of the wind through the ears of your horse, and it gives her comfort to think that if John could have chosen a way to go, this is what he would have wanted. A massive heart attack took him there and then.

Jess spoke at the funeral, in front of 250 people and at the age of just fifteen, to thank everyone for their support, and then she went and competed at the Boston Rowing Marathon barely a month later, having raised nearly £1,000 for the air ambulance that had taken him away. He wouldn't have wanted her to hang around, Sharon says. He'd have wanted her to press on, and she'd be making him proud.

One day, she's going to name a boat after her dad. She's going to call it *John Boy*, and she will get in it, and rip through the water like she used to tear around the field on the quad bike, or fly through the countryside on her horse, just like he did in his time; and he'll be a part of it all, like he always has been.

The Grind

"I think this might be my last season."

*

THIS PORRIDGE IS JUST RIGHT

Five? O' clock? In the morning? Sod that for a game of soldiers.

Six. 'sake. Back to sleep, come on now, you're not impressing anybody.

Seven. Hnnh.

Eight. Fine. *Fine.*

I'm up.

The sun rises, presumably, although it's a little hard to tell behind the thick banks of Mancunian cloud. It would be too cold for Carol Cooke, which is one way of making yourself feel better. It would be *way* too cold for Carol Cooke, who'd stay indoors at ten degrees higher, but it's good enough for a Scot in a few layers of Lycra and a waterproof Storey Racing top, and in any event John isn't going to let her off just because it's a bit nippy.

The start of December 2017 brings a double day of training, with a ride before lunch and then a RaceRun after. The ride's scheduled to last for between an hour and a half and two hours, and there are power and heart rate parameters to hit, but they're not too stringent because today is about fitness, not power. It's about keeping going.

Breakfast is the usual, a bowl of porridge with seeds of some sort, and then after a bit of pottering, it's 9.30ish and time to head out of Gatley Hall's patchily warm embrace, across to the garage to pick up Flash, her trusty training trike, and off and away. She tries to mix up the routes to keep things interesting, but today is going to be broadly familiar – down through Heald Green, past the prison at Styal, through Wilmslow, down towards Nether Alderley without even pausing for a snigger on the way past Dingle Avenue, and then round and back and home.

It doesn't take long before she needs to stop for a pee – there's the glamour of elite cycling for you – but there's a man who lives just off the route and has an outdoor bathroom, and he lets Hannah take a pit stop there if she needs to, so that's nice and convenient. He's watching the rugby league this morning. It's the World Cup Final, and England are playing. On the other hand, it's half time, and they haven't scored a point yet.

Back on the road, then, and one by one the houses drift away. The roads become a bit clearer, and everything's a few degrees quieter. But the aromas of fork are giving way to the odours of field, and the potholes are tending from bobbles to chasms, which means more concentration on the road than would be ideal. Above, planes roar through the mist on their way in to land at Manchester Airport, but there's not much mental bandwidth left for that as Hannah ticks off the pedal strokes, one, two, one, two. Just keep swimming, just keep swimming.

During most rides up in Glasgow, there'll be a comment or two from the sidelines – nothing significant, just a bit of inter-action. Here, there are some fleeting glances from passers-by, a moment or two of curiosity, but that's about it. With British Cycling being based just up the road, they're pretty used to cyclists.

Onwards. It's about 50 per cent of the effort she could put in if she really had to, perhaps a bit more, but after a tick over 32km and a hair under a couple of hours, that's enough for today. John has put together a rough training plan for the year which Hannah can access online, and at the moment, she's slap bang on track.

Back home, the first priority is a protein shake that tastes a bit like Nesquik but quite a bit more not like Nesquik, and an M&S cookie that goes down a little bit easier. And it's taken a while, but she's come to realise that what she needs to do after that – what's best for her – is to just sit.

To do nothing.

Because sometimes, being an Olympian isn't about doing more, about pushing harder or going for longer. In a few days' time, in fact, she'll pull up American para track and fielder Lex Gillette on just that point. "Doing just enough," Lex has tweeted, "is never an option when you're pursuing greatness." Which at first sounds lovely and motivational, but on reflection, kind of makes you wonder: if doing enough isn't actually enough, then what is? So Hannah chips in. "Actually," she says, "I've finally learnt that doing just enough to keep yourself from decking it, over to the edge of fatigue, is the point. Find where your just enough is and stick at it. Consistency. The porridge that was just right – you get me?"

Perhaps he does – he likes the tweet, at least – and it's a message which seems to strike a chord within the British cycling community, so Hannah elaborates. "Plan," she replies to a man who asks how she finds where her "just enough" is. "If you try to escape the plan, it's too much. If you're constantly dreading it, it's too much. I value external eyes – if you stop socialising, it's too much." But though she went out for a drink with some friends the other day, she won't be mentioning that on social media. Even if, in deference to her status as an athlete, it would have been very much in moderation, she doesn't want anything to jeopardise her chances of getting back on programme with British Cycling.

Not that there's a realistic prospect of that any time soon. As far as she knows, the key criterion for being taken back onto the British Cycling squad will remain as the percentage rule for the foreseeable future, so nothing's going to happen until next autumn at the earliest. But she's hanging on to the thought that last year they took a few riders to the world championships who had won silvers and bronzes at world cups, and so if she can win a medal or two at Ostend in May or Emmen in July, they might take her to Maniago in August – off-programme but riding for Great Britain – and then maybe a good showing there will change some minds.

Back to the present. After a bit more refuelling, some tomato soup and toast, it's a quick drive down to Woodbank Park, the home of Stockport Harriers & Athletic Club, for half an hour or so of RaceRunning. She's been keeping that side of things going in part because it's a change from her other training, but there's been some big news on that front recently too, with World Para-Athletics announcing that it's going to be included within the European Championships in the autumn of 2018. It'll be at least 2024 before it can work its way up to full Paralympic status, but for the time being Hannah remains world record holder in her RR3 category at every distance between 100 and 1500 metres and she's kept in touch with the relevant people behind the scenes, so she's going to be invited to the Europeans, and she's going to be competitive at the very least. And maybe, in a few years' time, she could be a multiple, multi-sport Paralympic champion.

But for now, round and round the track she goes, headphones pumping out something with a good strong beat, something that helps her block everything else out and just keep on churning through. And then home, rest and recover, dinner, a bit of studying, a snippet of a film, and then bed by 10.30.

Another day.
  Another day closer to Tokyo.

*

SNAP!

Bloody flu.

British Rowing's pre–Christmas camp is in Majorca this year, and it's a positive one for Jess, with a personal best or two in testing. There's a lot of indoor work – they were meant to be going quite heavy on the cycling, but it's chucking it down for most of the fortnight they're there and the tarmac on the roads has quite a lot of marble in it, so within the first day or two, a couple of the squad have already taken tumbles, including Beth, who's done something unpleasant to her back. So the coaches switch things around to keep them inside a bit more, doing longer and longer ergo runs, and they seem to be happy that no–one has missed out on much. There's some wind–down time at the end of the camp, including an awards ceremony where Jess, thanks to some quite spectacular faces pulled during the team–building tug–of–war, gets recognised as the squad's official "Best Gurner", and all in all it's good fun.

Then comes the British Rowing Indoor Championships, a multi–format ergo–a–thon in which Jess and her relay team come second, but which would probably pass without further comment except that one of the other competitors is former cycling royalty, in the body of Sir Bradley Wiggins. There's some talk of him trying to qualify for Tokyo 2020 as a rower, and, let's be honest, he's the sole focus of interest to the outside world at the Lee Valley VeloPark on this Saturday December morning, but he struggles a bit at the start of his men's open weight 2k, and even with double Olympic champion James Cracknell in his camp, it looks like a bit of a stretch.

Meantime, the flu is going through the squad, and it's run straight into Jess. She's had some blood tests, which haven't shown anything, and she's on protein and vitamin D supplements to help with recovery, but she keeps feeling under the weather, and she's disappointed to come in fifth at the trials assessment that falls just before Christmas, behind Vicky, Holly, Mathilda and Melissa Wilson, who only started rowing at university a couple of years back, but came fourth at the Worlds in the pair.

So over Christmas, homework is alternating days of a 12k and weights, then just a 12k, then 12k and weights again, and then another 12k. And it's still too much, it seems, because she doesn't feel great over New Year, and then after one day back in training, the flu comes properly roaring back, and she can't fly out to Avis for the next camp with the rest of the squad. Still, neither can Beth, who's got ill too on top of her back injury, so at least they can meet up.

It's a short burst this time for Jess, so Avis is back on, a week late but can't be helped, and at last, *at last*, through training and resting and training and resting, it starts to feel like the illnesses are under control. A few weeks back at home while the training starts to ramp up, and then out they all go to Seville in mid-February for another training camp and she's back on the full programme. Success! There are a few really good sessions with the full quad, Paul Thompson's really happy, and everything's looking good for a triumphant return to the Women's Eights Head of the River in early March.

After the ups and downs, the stops and the starts and the set-backs, it's a relief to think that finally, she can get in a long stretch of full-bore training, to properly set herself up for trials and for the seas-

– snap! –

Fuck's sake.

*

HOTELS AND HANDLEBARS

It's the early spring of 2018, and Hannah is due to go to the first world cup of the season in around seven weeks' time. She's got enough money to live, and that's great, but right now, she doesn't have enough money to race.

She's confident it'll all be fine, one way or another, but there are wheels within wheels. For one thing, Storey Racing are waiting on British Cycling before they can chip in, because there's a suggestion that the latter might want to take Hannah to Ostend. Not because they're getting her back on programme – not yet, anyway – but because results this season will count towards qualification spaces for the Paralympics. It's a tad complicated, but in essence, there's a big pot for women's road racing, and another one for women's track, and the same again for the men, and anyone who can finish in a top ten this season in a sufficiently high-level race will earn their country some points which, in the long run, can be put towards taking more people to Tokyo. And Hannah, who's fourth in the world or thereabouts in her classification, is potentially worth a lot of points – more, in all likelihood, than they would need to "spend" down the line to take up a women's road racing place – so this year, the word is that they're going to try to take her to Ostend.

The problem with that for now, though, is that it's still just a rumour. And with less than two months until the race, Hannah needs to start booking things.

But what?

She could fly to Belgium, but she needs to get her trike out there somehow too, and practically speaking, that's only going to happen if someone else can drive it, and who's that going to be? She could drive herself, but a full tank of petrol – which is roughly what she needs for the journey – will cost about the same as the flight, plus she needs to fork out for a ferry, and the whole arrangement gives her less time preparing at the venue, and more time sat behind a wheel, ahead of a race in which she could really do with picking up a medal. On the plus side, it would save her the £90-odd cost of an extra night at the race hotel – because when it comes down to it, that's where the real money goes. Is it worth it? The hotel's right next to the course, and it's got a gym on site – so if you can afford it, it's a massive help. If you're struggling, though, you're probably going to have to take your chances with Airbnb. And meanwhile, Hannah can't really book anything at all until she knows whether British Cycling will take her or not; and the longer she waits, the more prices start to jack up and hotels book out.

At least she's still got the Storeys in her corner. They've recently confirmed her on this season's squad, and Sarah said some lovely words about her at the team launch; and then they took her away to Lanzarote for a training camp too, which hadn't been part of her plan, but worked out very nicely indeed. "It really has a huge impact on me, training in the warm weather," she says. "With cerebral palsy, my muscles function better in the heat." What's more, it's a break from her normal surroundings and the day-to-day stresses, although it's not short of some anxiety of its own.

For one, she couldn't take Flash, her training trike. She'd been planning to. She'd packed everything else, and the last thing to do was to take his back wheels off for transit, and they wouldn't come off. So she went to a mechanic, and they still wouldn't come off, and she called around all her trike mates for help, and they still wouldn't come off. So she took Phoenix, the racer, instead, and thank goodness he didn't puncture, because she only had one set of tyres.

But it was lovely. She made friends with the owners of a

local bike shop, who said that they would rescue her if she got stuck in the middle of nowhere, and in return she let them ride Phoenix, and the guy was a former mountain biker himself, so he was really good at it, and he loved it. The rest of the team did their own thing, because Hannah by her own admission can't keep up with an able-bodied septuagenarian on a two-wheeler let alone the toned and honed elite, except then one day they came out for a casual ride on their rest day while Hannah was doing efforts. "They stayed with me, they shouted for me, I felt a lot safer so I could go a lot harder, and it was incredible," she says. "But it was kind of tinged with sadness. I'm pushing myself all the time, but you can only do so much alone.

"I went on a camp with British Cycling once, to Valencia, and Craig Collis-McCann, my trike team mate, and I were doing these five minute efforts on the road. It was great, because you could just go with another trike. But now, I don't really get that, ever."

And British Cycling don't end up taking her to Ostend. But she cobbles together some money from Storey Racing, and from a bit of tutoring that she's doing on the side, and she puts it down on a nice little place that she's found through Airbnb.

She'll be trying out some new handlebars too, thanks to a couple of guys called Mike Ellis and Charles McCulloch, who are local to Manchester, free to work with Hannah now and happy to work with her for free, and the latter used to hold the hour record[1] in the 50–54 age group and the former builds illegally fast bikes for fun, so they're good folk to have around.

---

1. An iconic part of the track cycling pantheon, about which there is plenty of excellent literature, but which for present purposes can be simplified to: Get on a bike. Ride round and round and round a velodrome for an hour, as fast as you can. Stop.

She's trained well, she's as strong as she's ever been, and she's going for a medal.

*

GAVIN

In a little pocket on the western Scottish coast, just southwest of Glasgow and within squinting distance of the Isle of Arran, sits the town of Ayr. A couple of streets back from the beach there's a house, and behind that there's a lane. And if Hannah Dines wins gold for Great Britain at the Tokyo Paralympics, it is a medal that will have been forged on that lane, by a tiny five-year-old Scottish boy and his parents, in the hours and hours and hours and hours that they spent pounding it down to dust, two little legs and a three wheeler.

When she was small, Hannah had been a pirate. She'd felt the rocking of the deck in her lack of balance and co-ordination, and the high winds and the rum-stupor through the muscles in her legs, torso and left arm, which her cerebral palsy kept unusually tight.

At the age of eight, she'd been asked to write about a favourite place that she had visited, and so she'd written about her bed. She had the top bunk, and a slide which her little sister wasn't allowed to use, which she could pull herself up with her arms and then scoot down, and that was brilliant; but more important, she could also lie down and enjoy the sensation, however brief, of being in control of her body. And she could dream of flying the bed out of the window and out to sea, to a school of magic and piracy – Hogwarts, if Harry had been Jim Hawkins. "If I could stay in my bed forever," she wrote, "I would."

That attachment passed, but she never forgot the sense of freedom. When she went on holidays, she would watch her sister splashing and somersaulting, and playing with the local children, and she would feel every bit of difference. That was why she had written about her bed – a place where she couldn't walk, but she could fly.

As the years passed, she did physiotherapy, reluctantly. "The thing was: you can walk, you can do stairs," she says. "Before sport, the physios in my life seemed so patronising. I mean, they were amazing, and they were trying to get me some level of independence, but you don't see it like that when you're a kid. So I just shied away from anyone trying to give me numbers of reps to do with my legs. 'No, you're patronising me, you're making me feel different.'"

All of which meant that if you'd told Margaret, her mother, back then that one of her children would become an international athlete, and you'd asked her which, it wouldn't have been Hannah, despite the fact that she'd always had a determined streak coupled with levels of concentration bordering on the obsessional. "She would be sitting and doing a jigsaw puzzle, or building something complicated out of Lego," says Margaret. "And most children would do a bit of Lego for two minutes, and then they'd rush off and do something else. But she would just stay there – she could stay there for an hour, even as a two-year-old."

There were flashes of physical enjoyment, of release. "They used to have a game in the playground," Margaret recalls. "Hannah would be at the front, and someone would hold on to the back of her Kaye walker, and then everyone else would make a crocodile behind her. I remember seeing them all running around the playground – there were about sixty kids, because everybody had joined in – and everybody was laughing, and I don't suppose she was running very fast, but she was running. But the idea of being able to excel at something physical? I think that just wasn't part of her childhood at all."

So she finished off at school, and off she went to university, to study physiology.

Gavin Drysdale is 17 years old now, with ataxic cerebral palsy that *affects his speech, coordination and balance. Twelve years ago, his parents took him along to a therapy centre run by cerebral palsy charity Bobath Scotland, and a Belgian physiotherapist introduced him to a running bike.*

So he took it out onto the lane behind his house. It's a proper race track of a thing – 400 metres long or so and with a slight descent to lend some momentum, even if Gavin's house, alas, sat at the foot of the incline, so he first had to soldier up before he could scamper down. Because that's what he wanted. Again and again, an ever-increasing intensity, a desperation to beat his top speed or his quickest time, picking the best line to avoid the gutters.

It wasn't really about racing at first, but the days passed and he kept it up, and as he explored the lane and the cycle paths dotted around the neighbourhood his parents would walk alongside him, and then they would jog, then they'd have to run, before finally resorting to bikes of their own, simply so they could keep up with their son.

The need to cycle in order to keep pace with an eight-year-old triggered something in Margaret and Peter Drysdale, and it wasn't long before they were looking around for competition – which proved problematic at first, given that not only were there no races in Scotland, they also couldn't find a single other person in the country with a running bike. They made enquiries at sports clubs, to be met by blank faces and furrowed brows, until at long last, having branched out their searches overseas, they stumbled upon Denmark.

And so in 2010, off they sent Gavin, to the annual RaceRunners Camp and Cup in Copenhagen. He needed to train in the build-up, so they persuaded the council to allow him to use the municipal athletics track. Janice Eaglesham, the de facto first lady of Scottish disability sport, took note, suggested that he enter a junior competition to record some times, and was impressed – so much so that she invited him to train with the wheelchair racers at the Red Star Athletics Club that she had set up with husband Ian Mirfin, and became his coach.

If Copenhagen was first and foremost a learning experience for a boy of Gavin's age – finding out what spikes were, discovering the Danish for "on your marks, set, go",[2] that sort of thing – two age group world records indicated that he had serious athletic promise. And he in turn didn't want to wait another year before racing again, so he convinced Margaret and Peter to set up the ACE RaceRunning Club – the first of its kind in the UK. Within two years, the club had picked up ten regular members, with clubs in Glasgow and Perth getting started as well and Margaret and Peter fielding a couple of enquiries a week through its website.

And in due course, a student with no sporting experience but an abundance of enthusiasm got in touch. "I definitely have a need for speed," she wrote, "and I have always dreamed of running easily." So Margaret and Peter wrote back, and within a few weeks a 19-year-old Hannah Dines was down at the club and taking her first steps on a RaceRunner.

As with Gavin, it became clear very quickly that she was very good – straight into the national team alongside him, representing Scotland at the 2013 International Wheelchair and Amputee Sports Federation World Games in the Netherlands, setting world records of her own, until cycling suddenly came along.

That was tough for Gavin to comprehend at first – they were only getting started in RaceRunning, and there was so much else to achieve – and it wasn't an easy decision for Hannah either. But RaceRunning, at least for the foreseeable future, wasn't a Paralympic sport, and cycling was.

2. "Klar! Parat! Start!" Don't say I don't teach you anything.

She kept in touch with Gavin, turning up when she could to watch him race, and stayed an ambassador for RaceRunning, crowbarring it into interviews that were supposed to be about cycling, and helping with the scientific research that needed to be undertaken in order for the International Paralympic Committee to consider introducing it as a Paralympic event.

And with its adoption as of January 2018 onto the World Para-Athletics circuit, maybe it soon will be. For now, Hannah is straddling both sports, while Gavin has been selected to represent Scotland at the CP World Games in August 2018, and is pushing towards the European Championships in Berlin that start a few days later. His training has dropped off a bit – he's still at school, he's got exams to do – but it's a balance he's trying to strike, and now, thanks in large part to the efforts of him and his parents to get RaceRunning recognised, he might one day be a Paralympian too.

"There is still a long way to go," he says. "Change is slow. But with each day that passes, it feels like we are getting closer."

*

TRAINING ON THE EDGE

It's another broken rib. The same as last year, the same as pretty much everyone had, but on the other side this time. It's turning out that part of gaining experience seems to be recognising injuries you've picked up before and getting ahead of them a bit quicker, and the good thing about this one is that Jess isn't trying to cycle or train through it like she did last year; but it still means a few more weeks out of the boat, a bit less time working on quadcraft with the others. A few weeks away from doing all Jess really wants to do right now, which is get in a boat, and row.

"You're constantly training on a knife-edge," she says, "and I seem to be getting it wrong quite a lot at the moment. I'm just hoping that these experiences now are going to help me train as consistently as I can, and make sure after each warning that I won't make the same mistakes again. This time? Yes, I've got another rib injury, but I honestly don't feel like I could have done any more to prevent it. I was doing my exercises, I put my hand up[3] as soon as anything hurt. And I know what I need to keep working on."

Because it's not binary, of course – injured or not injured, healthy or sick. You're almost always carrying something, even if most of the time it's pretty minor. Add it all up, in fact, and you're probably fully fit about twice a year, if you're lucky; and so unless you're properly injured or ill when a competition or an important assessment comes around, you'll take your chances. Like at Trakai in 2013, when Jess won her junior world gold with a strapped-up shoulder; or at the Under-23s just after Rio, which she raced with a(nother) broken rib. To be honest, you'll push through anything if you have to, she says;

3. Not sure that was the best idea.

you'll get into the boat not knowing what state you're going to be in when you climb out at the other end.

The problem is, though, that right now the coaches won't let her. She's on the mend, but rehab's dragging on, and so she gets pulled from trials relatively early. But then Mathilda goes down with a virus which keeps her out of action for the best part of two months; and they're the lucky ones. Holly's still having issues with her bladder and Beth's back problem has turned out to be pretty serious, so both of them are going to be out for the season.

If that's a blow after such a promising end to 2017, what might make it worse is that for the moment, there's not obviously much else behind them. Vicky is pushing ahead with her single. Alice Baatz has stepped on and is sculling a lot better this season, but she's struggling to translate that into efficiency in a crew boat, while Lucy Glover, for all her promise, is yet to make a real senior-level breakthrough.

But there are, at least, a couple of new faces.

One is quite similar to an old one – Melissa Wilson, by her own admission, is basically Holly. She's recently come over from the sweep side after taking up the sport at university and winning the Boat Race last year with Cambridge, but there's only about a second between her and Holly's ergo times, and style-wise, she reckons she'll be offering similar things in the boat. They're even, apparently, distantly related.

The other new face really is an old one – muscling in amongst the fresh-faced twenty-somethings this year, a 32-year-old Olympic silver medallist. Zoë Lee, who missed the entirety of 2017 after knee surgery, has a bit of history in the quad, but that amounts to two fourth places at world cups in 2013, and otherwise she's spent her professional career in sweep. She's back now, though, and it's a hugely different boat from five years back. "I was in the quad back then purely because it was the bottom boat," she says. "It was the year I broke into the team. Back then we all had to do a certain amount of sculling up until February anyway, and I was towards the bottom of the squad, so I was hovering in and out of the quad and around the bottom of the eight." This time round, though, it's all change. For one, Zoë's surgery meant that she missed the 2017 World Championships, and that meant that she had to do the first open assessment, right at the beginning of the year in October, and she had to do it in a single. She'd had a bit of practice – a year's solo rehab had left her in a single scull more often than not – and then when she won it, that caught the eye of the coaches. There were big ideas that they might test her out against the 2017 crew, but Zoë got ill in December, and then a couple of others were ill in February, and then everyone missed out in April, so it never really happened. But in the meantime, she kept punching up at the top of the bunch that were racing, so she stayed in the conversation.

There was also the question of familiarity. Post-Rio, there'd been a big turnover on the sweep side, but Jess and Mathilda had been around for a while, she knew a bit more about them, and frankly, she wanted in with the girls that had the experience, and who – what's more – were starting to win medals. She won't admit to a preference between sculling and sweep, but she sounds enthusiastic now. "I'm really, really enjoying having the opportunity to try something different," she says. "And ultimately for me, I learnt to row in an eight. I think I know quite a lot about big fast boats now, and with the quad being quite a big fast boat, I think there's quite a lot of transferable knowledge."

So May comes around with Zoë and Jess training in a double, waiting for a couple of others to stay fit enough to fill out the rest of a quad. The first world cup, in Belgrade, comes too early for that, but the plan was always to do only two of the three world cups this year anyway, to avoid making the racing season too long or too full, so they'll just go to Austria's Linz-Ottensheim and to Lucerne instead – assuming, of course, that there are enough functional limbs to put a boat together.

*

END OF THE ROAD?

It's 14th May 2018. The Ostend World Cup was a little over a week ago. Hannah came fifth in the time trial, three minutes and 33 seconds back from Carol and well off the times set by Jill, Monica and Jana; and she came fifth in the road race too, 3:47 shy of a gold-medal shootout in which Jill pipped Carol on the line, with Monica half a minute back and Jana somewhere in the middle.

The conversation took something of a turn.

Hey.

Hey.

How's it going? How was the racing?

Good. Really good.

It was crazy, actually. We got there, Mike and Charles and me, about ten o' clock in the evening two days before the time trial. And then the day before, we went out to train on the course and it was super windy, and really cold. Nine degrees, winds coming in from the Netherlands, and I couldn't even control the bike, which was really scary. So I was like, oh god, I'm doomed. I can't even hold it in a straight line.

But then the race day was super calm, no wind, you could hear a pin drop. Gently warm, and just perfect. And we had a plan, and I followed the plan, except—

Well, ah.

So, I was really organised, and I got my timetable together, and we were all looking at it, we all had our own roles, you know, set up, bike check, pump up the wheels, that sort of thing. And Mike and Charles had both checked it, and everyone was happy, and then Mike goes off to stand somewhere on the course and Charles comes with me to the start.

And we see everyone starting, and oh look, that's a woman starting, and we're like, huh, that's weird. They shouldn't have gone off yet, I should get there before that. And it turns out I've got about a minute to spare before my start time, because I've got all the timings wrong by ten minutes. Then I couldn't get past the spectators, because the pavements were really narrow, and then I had to get past all these trikes – and in the end, I didn't spend any time being nervous, because I just went straight up the start ramp, had 30 seconds looking at the start, and then I went.

It was great. We'd been practising my aero position, but we hadn't got me going in a straight line, and I kept coming off aero bars in England, because a lorry would come past, or the camber would be off, or there would be a pothole, and I just couldn't get the powers up. So we were thinking I couldn't use aero bars, but John, my coach, was saying, just keep them on. If you can't use them, you can't use them, no bother.

So there they were, and I gave them a try, and it went really well. I was on the aero bars, I felt super strong, it felt really good not to be battling the wind as hard. I was pushing out a huge power, and I was looking like my other competitors, I was in their image.

What was the course like?

There was a technical bit and another bit that was just out and back, and the time trial started on the technical bit. And that was really hard, the corners were really poor as usual – in my mind, there's just nothing I can do about my brain, it just stops as soon as I reach a corner. We've tried and we've tried and we've tried, but I just don't have the motor function. I've worked on it year after year, and yes, I've seen a little bit of development, but I can't come off the saddle, because I can't stand on one leg, and I can't get back on the saddle if I come off.

I thought that I would get powerful enough to overcome that, but I haven't. I also thought that when I had a crossbar trike, which I do now, that I would be able to use the crossbar to corner. And I can't. And I was really riding on that. That was my hope. But my brain is just letting me down. I can squat huge loads, I can push myself to the max; but set against that, I can't stand up on a trampoline. I can't walk backwards. Because I have brain damage in that area, of proprioception and body co-ordination. And that's not a requirement in trike racing, you just have to have some spasticity.

But the acceleration was good, and then we got on the out-and-back stretch. And then, there were two laps, it's a longer course that they went for in the end, an 18km one, which was a point of debate right up until the day before.

How come?

There's a rule book, a UCI rule book on para-cycling, and for every competitor, they have a set distance they can do in the race. So each city that wants to host a para-cycling race looks at the rule book and picks a route within the limits of the distance. And mine is 15km. And they picked a distance which was 18km, which is obviously significantly different, and they did this for every discipline. They went way over for every-body.

They always have a managers' meeting beforehand, and they had a vote at the managers' meeting to ask whether they should keep the distances or not. But of course, the only real options were either doing one lap – so 9k – or two, and normally, you'd expect a race to be between 11 and 15km, so it was really quite annoying. But anyway. It was achievable.

On the second lap, Jana caught me. She was there, she'd made up a minute on me by the start of the second lap, but I didn't let up, so I only let her get away by ten seconds more over the second half of the race. And I paced it really well, I hit my maximum power over both laps. So actually, it was an incredible effort, it really went well, it was exactly how I wanted it. Like last year, with John, it still went really well, but of course I wasn't on aero bars, so there was a big difference in how I did.

But for all that, it was still fifth, with a humungous gap to the podium. And that was a real shock. This year was my dream race – even in terms of the rush at the start. That's actually a really good tactic, you don't want to stand around for fif-teen minutes getting cold, even if I did get a big fine from the UCI – about £75 or so in Swiss francs. So the prize money's not equal across genders, but the fines are! Although that said, there's no prize money for any of our races in Belgium. People won a bottle of beer if they got on the podium, and that's it. Some competitions, they do give you money, some don't, but it's not really that much anyway, it's the equivalent of about £20.

So anyway, with this perfect effort, I still came fifth, and it was a really big smack in the face. Because, essentially, I believed that I could bridge the gap in our classifications by my huge powers and my perfect time trial position. And it was a really big win in terms of my powers. Huge, bigger than it had been before on aero bars. To put it into some context, last time I did a race with aero bars, I was averaging around 130 to 140 watts. That was last year. Then this time on aero bars, I averaged 160 watts. So that's a huge leap.

But it got me fifth. It got me 30 seconds closer to gold, but otherwise the same as I came last year. Which was hugely disappointing. It was a perfect day and a perfect race, but the podium was exclusively over-50, and that was as big a shame to me – because Jana's me. I mean, she's a little bit more able-bodied than me, for sure, she doesn't have the same issues in her legs and her torso, but she is more my image, and she is more my age. And she's been doing this for eight years now. But she got pushed back into fourth place, so she's now out of the medals, and it's just depressing when you see that.

How about the road race?

Well, road racing is interesting, because I do have a little bit more of a chance. But this road race in Belgium, it really wasn't for me at all, it was very, very left hand dominant, and really, really corner-y. There was an out-and-back stretch, but essentially it was all corners.

And just like last year, I got dropped on all the corners, but I managed to make it back up – and it was so much easier than last year. I could do my own efforts at a huge pace, and also keep up with Carol's efforts as well, and then do my other attacks. I've never felt that powerful. I've never felt that I can actually be in the game when Carol goes off on a sprint. And that was really cool.

The problem was that it was four laps. I had to lead the technical section, the whole technical section, because I'm the only slow one on corners out of Jana and all the rest. But going into the third lap, I was on the back of the bunch, so I had to sprint to get on the front, and there wasn't enough room, and I just didn't make it. So I got off the back, and once I was off the back and they were so fast at cornering, then that was it.

In one sense, it's an improvement, because in Belgium last year, I wasn't even in the road race at all. But even so, we finished with essentially exactly the same distances between us as the time trial, except for Jill beating Carol to gold.

The problem is, physically I'm not what Jill and Carol and Monica are – and possibly not Jana either. I'm not that far off their power outputs, but I'm inefficient, because of my wonky legs. We've tried to adjust for that with splints, but it's still not anywhere close to how efficient the others are, what cadences they can produce and at what powers.

But on the other hand, I'm not a T1 – at least, not with things as they are. I mean, obviously there's a wide range of different privileges that give people different strengths, and different genetic traits, and that's fine, but it's not like there are fine margins in this sport – it's minutes rather than split-seconds. Maybe there can be three classifications in the future – Jill messaged me before Ostend, and we're going to email someone at the UCI at some point so maybe they can roll it out – but is that going to be in my timeline? So realistically, I will never be in a classification that suits me in cycling. We're going to send an email, once we've worked out who to send it to, but for me, now, I want a medal. I want to be successful. So it's bringing up a lot of questions for me.

What sort of questions?

Ok, so don't get me wrong here, because this is a very complicated situation. It's very emotionally confusing. I talked to John about my performance, and he said, there are things that you can improve. So I asked him, what exactly, can you tell me specific things? And he said that I wasn't very smooth on the out-and-back section, but then he looked at it on WKO4, which is his data analysis tool,[4] and I had 0.5 smoothness, which is really good, that's what the pros have. And I had 0.4 heart rate to power, which is about how much your heart rate varies, how fit you are, because if you're not used to it your heart rate will just climb, and so that was pretty much perfect too. My acceleration was huge, and all in all, he said, that performance should have got me bronze. He thought that would get me bronze. And it didn't.

And I used to be fine with developing and just being an athlete, but now I'm not. I want to come and set the scene. I've always wanted to be the strongest person with cerebral palsy, and I can't do that with cycling, because British Cycling won't give me the chance. They won't fund me, they won't take me to specific events, so eventually, I need to change my focus.

I don't know – right now, I've still got funding for the next race, and it still might be possible there. But if it isn't possible this season and I have given it everything that I could possibly give it, then is this where should I put my energy?

I never thought I would be in this situation. I thought that, with hard work, four years of good training all the time, I could be pushing for gold. But if I don't get funding this year, and I don't get to go to the world championships, and I don't get to train with other trikes, then my development will just get more and more stunted. I'm missing my team mates like anything, and I can't do it without them and I don't want to do it without them. And that was never going to happen this year,

---

4. www.trainingpeaks.com/wko4.html, if you're curious.

but I wanted a bronze just to keep me going. There were little things that were going to keep me going, and they're not there. And if John can't give me a guide to bronze, and to getting back on squad, then he's just giving me empty belief.

What do other people think?

Some of my closest friends have said I should just switch, and go all out on RaceRunning. It's so difficult, because I'm not a quitter. I can't do it, it's not in my blood, it's not what I want to do. But at the rate I'm improving at the moment, it would take me seven years to catch up with Carol, and that's if she doesn't get better herself. And I can't afford – physically, mentally, financially – to give the same effort for seven years without some sort of reward.

I'd have to replace it with something, though – I can't stop being an athlete, and I want to be a champion. I want to get gold.

So I'm still very undecided, and I've still got funding for this next race – and maybe Belgium's just not the race for me, and Emmen might be. But I think this might be – it might be – my last season.

Shit.

*

SIXTY SAUSAGE ROLLS

If Nottingham showed that Jess had something that could be worked with, there was plenty she still needed to improve. A picture from the podium summed it up – there she was, standing on the highest block, right in the middle, and there were the other girls, the silver and bronze medallists, and they were just towering over her.

You've got to get stronger, Ian said. It wasn't really the done thing to encourage weight training at such a young age, but Ian kept a close eye on her, and she took it all on board, because she wasn't going to let size keep her down. She wanted to row, and she wanted to win. To do that, she needed to get stronger, so that's what she would do.

To develop her stamina and toughen her up, Ian suggested that she take part in the club's weekly 9k time trial – every Saturday, eight a.m. sharp. She did, and because she was a 14-year-old girl up against adults, she'd come last, but at least she was out there doing it.

And they muddled along together, Ian and Jess, step by step. What's the next challenge? What's the next race, and how do we go about preparing for it? Trial and error, onwards and upwards. They added in extra training, so while most of the other youngsters at the club were doing four sessions a week, Tuesday, Thursday, Saturday, Sunday, Jess would be going for a double session on Saturdays, another double on Sundays, Monday night, Tuesday night and Thursday night, and then Wednesday night weights on top of it all, with the club empty save for the two of them working away, building her up.

Trial and error. Ian had a couple of guiding principles – keep your technique the same on the ergo and on the water; and if it looks right, it probably is – and eventually Jess found her way onto British Rowing's radar, at which point a couple of the junior coaches, Richard Boulton and Ade Roberts, started coming to see her, and

Ade watched her one day and said to Ian, she's not using her hips. What do you mean, asked Ian, she's not using her hips? And Ade said, well, she's not driving through with the hips; and Ian had rowed for the best part of thirty years and he'd never driven through with his hips in his life. But Ade showed Ian on the ergo, and Ian showed Jess, and she started going even faster.

They put her in quads for a couple of years, which was great, and bit by bit she kept building up her skills and building up her confidence, until it began to feel like, for one reason or another, the boats weren't quite getting the best they could out of the talent which was in them; and if Jess was going to fail, she wanted it to be on her own terms, and so she went for trials in 2013 and said, I don't really want to do a quad this year, I want to do a single.

And Jess and Ian kept on pressing Richard Boulton, and eventually, towards the end of a Hollingworth Lake 140th anniversary dinner at which everyone had had, shall we say, an extremely pleasant time of it, he promised that if she won in the single at the Munich Junior International Regatta, they'd let her race the single at the world championships. And she did – comprehensively – and a promise is a promise, so off she went to Trakai. And that went well.

After an international gold medal, there wasn't much prospect of Jess carrying on at Hollingworth Lake; but if he's honest, it broke Ian's heart a bit. There were all sorts of offers – scholarships at Harvard and Princeton, all over the place. But British Rowing said yes, you could do that, but it'd be better if you stayed in the system here, where we can keep an eye on you, and help you out.

And to this day, Jess and Ian have remained close. Over the years at the club, they'd developed a bit of a post-race routine – Ian's wife doesn't like him eating sausage rolls, and Jess's mum's a vegetarian, so after she competed, off they'd sneak to a Greggs and they'd each get a sausage roll – and so for Ian's 60th birthday, in early 2018, she bought him sixty of the damn things.

Had to give a lot of them away, though. They were even bigger than he is.

*

THE STRUGGLE CONTINUES

The results at the first world cup of the season don't come as a surprise. It's a top three of the Netherlands, Poland and Germany, which minus Great Britain is exactly how it finished at the World Championships, and most of them haven't done much to their crews. All in all, then, not a lot to give GB great pause for thought ahead of Austria, except that half of this year's lot are completely new to the boat and functionally new to sculling.

And so Mathilda, Jess, Zoë and Melissa head off to Linz, to race on the Danube in World Cup II. This regatta comes with a bit of added spice – Linz will be hosting next autumn's world championships, which will provide the first opportunity for boats to qualify for Tokyo, so this is a good opportunity for an early recce. Perhaps that's on the minds of other nations too, because suddenly there's a rush of entries, twelve boats in all.

Poland will be there again, ploughing on with the same foursome. The Dutch and the Germans have shaken things up a bit, while Australia, in pleasing news for fans of nominative determinism, have raided their 2017 World Championships bronze medal-winning double scull for a 25-year-old called Olympia Aldersey.

Perhaps the most interesting-looking boat, though, is the Belarusians. It's hard to know where their priorities lie – their crew is a combination of the two doubles that finished fifth and sixth in Belgrade, and the entry list has them down as racing in both events – but assuming they do end up doing the quad, it'll be the first opportunity that Jess will have had since a singles match-up before her junior worlds a few years back to go up against Ekaterina Karsten.

Karsten's results over the last couple of years have been a bit up and down, one way or another. Silver in the single at the Europeans last year, eighth in the same boat in Rio. At world championships level, she hasn't won a medal since a bronze in the double in 2013, and she hasn't won gold since 2009, when she was in her single.

On the other hand, she has won a couple of medals in the quad, including an Olympic bronze. And given that she picked that up at Barcelona 1992, and she's still competing at the top level 26 years later – well, best not to ignore her.

It ends up as, let's say, a learning experience. In the time trial that acts as the heat – World Rowing are testing out alternative racing arrangements just in case weather conditions at a regatta mean that not all of the lanes can be used – it's a struggle at the start. This crew has only been together for a few weeks – only a week or so in the seat order in which it's competing, in fact, and it hasn't even done a full 2k piece in training – and it's coming to terms with the fact that it's carrying a lot of raw power. In principle, it's great that this crew's ergo performances are so much better than last year's, but in practice, that means that if they get out of sync, things can go significantly wronger.

So they end up in the repêchage, which reverts to the normal race format, and again, they leave too much behind at the start. They trail in third, behind the Germans and the Australians, which leaves them in their first B final of the Olympiad.

And then, in that, they finally manage to step things up. The repêchage had been an improvement on the time trial, they all feel like the boat's come on a lot, but this is the result that the other countries might notice. They take first place comfortably, and although that leaves them in seventh overall, their time is the second quickest across both finals – and in what seems to have been less favourable weather conditions. Does it mean much that it's Germany who take the gold, from China and Australia, and that the Netherlands and Poland can only trail in fifth and sixth? It's hard to say – who knows what everyone's prioritising? – but as far as the British boat's concerned, it's an improvement.

Onwards to Henley.

And for the time being, we shall gloss over the elephant in the boat.

*

A CHANGE OF FORTUNE; AND A SMALL BOX
FILLED WITH STEAM

When the time came, shortly after the Ostend races, there didn't seem to be much point. Nothing v., nothing g., though, so Hannah applied for the world championships.

In truth, there really wasn't much point. The criteria for selection for Maniago were pretty unequivocal: riders who weren't on programme needed to have 'achieved a medal performance' in Ostend. Simple as that. In theory, there were a couple of catch-alls, but relying on her "personal conduct and attitude" allowing her to "contribute positively to the performance of the team and the team environment", or hoping that she might sneak in by way of "any other points that the selection panel deems necessary" seemed like a bit of a long shot.

But a long shot is still a shot, and so Hannah applied for the world championships. She wanted to know that she had done everything that she could, not least because Maniago – with its out-and-back time trial – is as close to the likely Tokyo course as she's going to get. On top of which, it's a convenient location – it's not South Africa, and it's not Canada, where the third world cup race is going to be, so it shouldn't be too much disruption, either financially or in terms of travel. But it's not going to happen, so there it is.

Except that of course, out of nowhere, it does.

Congratulations, they said. You've been selected, they said – but you're going to have to pay for your own travel and accommodation. Which was a bit disappointing. Great, of course, that they were planning to take her, but they would be paying for everyone else, so why did she have to find £1,275? Especially as – and this may sound familiar – she didn't have

£1,275. And she couldn't ask Storey Racing to fund it, because she wouldn't be racing for them. So Sarah suggested another crowdfunder.

It's only once in your life (you would hope) that someone joyrides your car into a petrol station and ends up torching the racing trike on which you've competed at a Paralympic Games shortly after you've been dropped by your sport's governing body – so back then, Hannah felt that crowdfunding was justified. But this feels different. This feels – to put it bluntly – like discrimination. In short, she would argue, British Cycling is a multi-million pound organisation. If they're prepared to pick her for Maniago, they should find the money to take her.

And this, in essence, is what she posts on Facebook, after Sarah has talked her into asking the public to dig a little deeper into their pockets. And that, in turn, gets people's backs up. It's an opportunity that you wouldn't normally have had, argues a fellow GB rider, and you didn't have to take it up if you didn't want to pay. It sounds like you're ungrateful, suggests British Cycling's performance director, Stephen Park, who asks her in for a meeting to discuss the way forward. It's not a disciplinary meeting as such – she's not on programme, they don't have the jurisdiction to sanction her – but if it goes badly, it's hardly going to help.

It could have gone a lot worse. Hannah's an emotional person – it's that emotion as much as anything which helps people to warm to her, and enabled her to knock off this latest crowdfunding target within an hour and a half – and she's holding herself in a bit as the meeting goes on. She doesn't agree with the stand that performance director Park – "Sparky", as he's almost universally known – is taking, when as far as she's concerned, there is money available if they wanted to pay it, but she doesn't press the point. She doesn't voice her real concern, which is: if they're going to treat her differently now, what's to keep them, irrespective of her performance at the world championships, from continuing to do so, from refusing to take her back? And she doesn't emphasise that she's also not just there for herself, she's there on behalf of other Hannahs, future Hannahs, Hannahs whose CP stops them being able to speak, Hannahs who might not have the same access to external support, or to crowdfunding.

But at least as far as this Hannah is concerned, it's opened up a line of communication with British Cycling that, for the last year or so, she doesn't feel like she's had; and what's more, there's a remark towards the end ("Let's see how you do at the world championships") that might have been no more than a throwaway, but which comes across to Hannah as a suggestion that maybe, if she can just put in a good showing in Maniago, she might get back on the squad, and not have to worry about all this crap for a while.

In the meantime, she's going to keep quiet, and put everything she can into training.

She decides not to race at Emmen, the season's second world cup. For one, having been selected for the world championships already, there's a strong case for focusing her energies on that, saving some money, and removing Emmen as a distraction. For another, there's been more upheaval within her inner circle.

She'd planned to meet up with Mike and Charles shortly after Ostend, to go through what had worked, what hadn't, and what they needed to improve on for the next race. The meeting got pushed back a bit while Hannah spent a week up in Scotland with her mum, but then they all met up at Mike's house, and it was really positive. This is how far you are away from gold; these are the things we can do, the non-physiological gains we can make, these are our ideas. Go away and talk to John about timings, and we'll meet up again.

So she went away, and she spoke to John, and a few days later, she heard about her world championships selection, and so she got Mike and Charles round to her place. Have you had a chat to John, they said; and Hannah said yeah, but he hadn't been super receptive, because they'd wanted to know exactly what he was going to do in terms of physiological improvements, in terms of coaching, to get her to close the gap, and John's not really like that. He's reluctant to open up about how he works and what he does, and he looks at things more on a week-to-week basis – here's where you are now, here's how I think you can do next week, this is what I want, I want you to aim for that.

So she tells Mike and Charles this, and it's not entirely clear why, but Mike goes quiet, and then says sorry, but he's out. This seems to come as a surprise to Charles – or so Hannah sees it – and there follows a tense conversation during which Hannah is trying to hold herself together, because she's been really invested in these two, who seemed so excited about working with her, and who've been helping her so much.[5]

As it happens, a few days later they recant a little, and say they're only pulling out until after the world championships, but Hannah's not quite sure what she thinks about people who make a commitment to her and then try to back out of it, even when they've been working for her for free and so have no real

---

5. They've been so good, in fact, and Charles has pulled so many bits and pieces out of his garage and helped Hannah put the lot together, that Flash and Phoenix are now essentially non-functional, skeletons cannibalised for parts, leaving Hannah with a third version that she has, of necessity, named Frankentrike. Frankie, for short.

obligation to her – and so it's not clear how this is all going to end. In the meantime, though, she won't be getting any advice on race position, or any mechanical time trial development, which is a big blow.

She will at least, however, be working on something new. The world championships have been scheduled for the hottest time of the year in Maniago, which means that it's going to be around 30°C, and 80% humidity. And the weather's been lovely in Manchester over the past couple of weeks, but that's not quite enough, so Hannah's going to do some heat training.

This can take a few different forms – it's part of why Jess goes on all those training camps with British Rowing. But Hannah, not being on programme, and not having the money to take herself off into the sun, is going to have to make do with sitting on a Wattbike in a small box filled with steam at Manchester Metropolitan University.

She's known about this for a while – the university's "environmental chamber", as they call it, can be engineered to provide temperatures from 50°C down to -40°C as well as depleted oxygen levels, so Sarah has used it to help her adjust to heat and altitude before. The day Hannah was selected, one of her team mates told her that the rest of the squad had been heat training for ages, and to get herself into a heat chamber as soon as she possibly could, so that's what Hannah's doing – although she's probably not quite going to get the full benefit.

The ideal approach would be to undergo what's known as "adaptation", which would involve fifteen straight days in the chamber, two hours minimum each day, and then another three days just before competition, so your body is fully attuned to the conditions it's going to face. That's not going to be possible for Hannah, though, because the MMU chamber isn't open every day, and what's more it's leaking and needs patching up; and so John's getting her on a programme of "familiarisation" instead. That's also fifteen days in the chamber, but with gaps in between, and trying different efforts and different temperatures while you're inside. "So my body's kind of used to the feeling, rather than actually being able to deal with it," Hannah says with a smile. The process is a happy blend of the technological and the old-school, as Hannah hooks herself up to a power meter and a heart rate monitor and then off she goes, while next to her a guy called Steve makes notes on a clipboard and every five minutes sticks a thermometer in her ear to check her body temperature and make sure she's not about to keel over.

The training comes with a couple of side-effects. On the plus side, heat is good for Hannah's muscles; against that, it makes her feet expand, which means that her hard carbon splints start to press into the flesh. The university have made her some splints that go outside her shoes, though, so hopefully that issue will resolve.

*

MORE CHOPPY WATERS

There's a loud bleep, and Jess pounds the water, again and again.

Tick.

Tick.

Tick.

And then, at last, the latest boat to have been trampled by the GB quad, the Norwegians, limps across the finish line. Three days of racing at Henley. Friday – Leander, beaten by more than four lengths. Saturday – Edinburgh University and Leander (basically, the GB Under-23s) beaten by 2¾ lengths. Sunday – Norway (racing as Christiania Roklub), beaten by three.

The yin; the yang. A week later, and the boat is scratched from Lucerne after the medical staff pick up another problem with Jess's rib, which leaves the quad's world cup season as one appearance, and no A finals. Which might not be a major problem in the long run, but it certainly wasn't the plan.

The yang; the yin. For Jess, a break from racing means a proper opportunity to catch up with her engineering course. She'd booked herself on to a week-long residency at Bath University back in January with the thought that there was never going to be a good time to do it, but with her injury it's turned out that now is as good a time as any. And so she's in the gym every morning at half six, and doing physio sessions, and fitting in trunk circuits or thirty minute squats sessions at lunchtime, and when lectures finish at five she gets a little break for dinner before more talks until nine at night. It's pretty full on.

Back on the water, there are two chances left this year. Two chances to work on race pace and rhythm, two chances to show something to the rest, two chances to sort things out.

Jess gets picked for the European Championships in Glasgow, and it's a matter of days beforehand when it's decided that the oedema on her rib isn't worth the risk. Alice gets roped in, so at least GB have brought a boat, and they put in a decent enough showing to finish in fourth place in the A final, but they're still struggling to get into the race. Jess talks to them afterwards and they're happy enough – they stayed close to the Dutch – but they're not keeping up their pace out of the blocks. Meanwhile, Ukraine are coming into the picture, Germany are going to offer a lot more again if they bring their proper crew to the worlds, and that's without even mentioning Australia or China or the Americans.

Before all of that, though, the crew are heading to France for another training camp, which brings them to the river at Temple-sur-Lot. There are some good set pieces, some first 100 metre drills, some first 300s, and a really exciting last day time trial where they do a full 2k run and finish top of percentage gold medal time – which they haven't done much this year – and Jess kills a catfish.[6]

It was dying anyway, or that's how she tells it. The catfish in this river are famous, they've been featured on the BBC's *Planet Earth*, they're that big – they eat pigeons! – and the quad are cranking out a rhythm, out and back and down and through, and then smack! – and the others are like, "It's a log, don't worry, it's a log," except Jess, who hit it, is like no, it's really not. I've hit logs, and that was very much a not-log, that was an animal. Coach Thompson looks back down the river. And sure enough, up gently floats a catfish, body intact but soul fluttering windward.

Then there's an angry French man who comes out in his

---

6. Author's note: Jess has asked me to emphasise that this was accidental. Which I had assumed anyway; her insistence, frankly, makes me start to wonder.

motorboat and chases down the eight because he thinks they're rowing too close to the bank, and then on the final night of the camp they have a quiz where Jess's team end up in the top two and have to go through a tiebreaker which involves a basketball shoot-out which in turn confirms that most of the British Rowing women's squad are quite definitely in the right sport, so all in all, you know, it's a good experience.

Then on to Italy, and more work fine-tuning the race plan. It's quite specific, it's been worked out by British Rowing as the best way to get the boat from A to B, and so however much you might need to react mid-race to what's going on around you, even that reaction's going to be shaped by the plan. By the eighth stroke of the race, for instance, they want to be up at maximum speed, and then it's about holding that for as long as possible. They tick off the distance, 100 metres by 100 metres, until about 300, when they'll be looking to have hit their rhythm. Then on top of that, there's a four-part race breakdown which they've characterised by way of emotions. For the first 500 metres, they want to feel fear; the next 500 is about feeling bold, the third 500 is passion, and the fourth is pride. Then on top of *that*, they're building for the line from 750 metres out, so it's 15 strokes on Mathilda's call, whatever that is, then another 15, then ten, ten, ten to the line.

Simple as that, really.

As long as they're all pulling together.

*

THE ONE WHERE MONICA NEARLY FALLS
DOWN A RAVINE

Race plans can, of course, take all sorts of different forms. There's the "hit it early and hang in there". There's "build and grind", "race the competition", "race the course". "Another rider nearly falling down a ravine halfway through the time trial and being unable to compete in the road race"? Ah, maybe not so much.

But Hannah's not going to put a caveat on two world championship fourth places. How she'll describe it, in fact, is as the best competition that she's ever been on with British Cycling – and that includes Rio. The team flies out a week and a half before racing starts, she's rooming with Karen just like the old times, and in between eat, train, sleep, eat, train and sleep, she manages to carve out a day with fellow GB triker Craig Collis-McCann, who takes her round the course with him and tells her how he'd do all the corners (not that it helps him, he cocks them up when he comes to race).

It's pelting down with rain the day before the women's time trial, which is a bit of a worry, but the morning dawns clear, and as it pans out, Hannah misses all the drama. She's been sent out first, up the hill through the village, twisting down, across the bridge over the ravine, up, down again and back through to Maniago. She's strong up the hill and careful on the descent, and Carol and Jill and Jana do it quicker but not by all that much, while Monica overcooks a corner and slams herself into the rocks. "That's part of bike racing," says Hannah. "I was careful on the downhill."

There's no real post-time trial recovery time, so Monica's out of the road race too, which takes place the next day in 39 degree heat. Which is fine – that's what the heat training was for, and heat is good for Hannah's muscles – but does bring up a side issue which she hadn't considered before. For most road cyclists, there's a simple response to hot weather – namely, your coach stands off to the side and chucks some cold water at you as you whizz past. For Hannah, with her CP and her heightened startle reflex – which means that when the water hits her, her muscles freeze, her head snaps back and for a few moments she stops pedalling – that's more of a problem.

But on she goes, and for a lap and three-quarters of the two lap course, she's right up there. She's staying on Carol's wheel, with the thought that she'll hang on there for as long as she can, and then once she can't do that any longer, she'll block Jana, and stop Jana getting in behind Carol. She's bashing into Jill, who's also pushing for the spot behind Carol even though, with her power, she doesn't really need to. And then Jill attacks, Carol goes with her, and Jana manages to nip in front of Hannah too. And then even that might have been ok, except that Hannah gets stuck with a group of male T1s.

This side-by-side racing – the more severely impaired men being sent out at the same time as the female T2s – happens sometimes. The expectation is that everyone will be going at a similar sort of pace, and you're allowed to work together, if you can. In this race, though, there's no-one Hannah can get on her side. If Rickard Nilsson, a fellow RaceRunner-triker, was here, they'd have two-upped it, and they might have caught Jana. He's not, though, so she talks to them all out on the road. "Come on, I'll pull you to the finish." But no-one goes for it – Hannah's strong, maybe they're worried that they'll burn out – and so Hannah ends up dragging the lot of them around the rest of the course until, with about 500 metres to go, with the effort they've saved while Hannah was doing all the work at the front, they scoot straight round her and sprint for the line

– which is a particular shame today, given that they catch Jana too.

Still.

A tiny bit more strength. An ounce of hill training. A friend in the pack. It feels like fine margins now.

But before she can get into the winter training season, a couple of weeks after Maniago comes the European Athletics Championships, which Hannah's been adamant that she'll compete in ever since RaceRunning was confirmed on the World Para-Athletics calendar. British Athletics takes a huge team to Berlin – over fifty athletes – and that means that there's room not only for Hannah, but also fellow Scot Kayleigh Haggo, Sheffield-based up-and-comer Rafi Solaiman, and… Gavin Drysdale. It feels like a homecoming, with Gavin, and Janice Eaglesham, and some of Hannah's first ever sporting team mates; but a little unexpectedly, it also brings home just how much she's changed. "It kind of made me feel a bit evil," she says. "I've been changed by performance sport. The others are still very team-orientated, and they want to hang out, you know, enjoy the experience. Whereas now, I just go straight in there – one goal, did that, kept myself to myself."

Gold medal, check. New world record. Check. Which of course brings the question back – can you carry on doing both? Would you want to double up, if RaceRunning was in the Paralympics in 2024? Maybe she'll change her mind later, but for now, the answer's pretty unequivocal. "No. I wouldn't do both. I want to give RaceRunning what it deserves, which is an athlete dedicating a whole Olympiad, or more, to it. And anyway, I wouldn't be doing my physiology any good, with trike racing being endurance and RaceRunning being sprint."

Fair enough. So it's back on the road.

She's emailed British Cycling. As soon as she finished at the world championships, in fact, literally the day after the road race. Do they think her performances warrant consideration for programme funding? That's been the goal, after all, and what with a recent funding fuck-up, the matter has become rather pressing.

Last year, as she describes it, she was hunted down by the Winning Students people. They gave her all the information and told her when to apply. They've lined her up for next year as well, but this year – not sure quite how – the deadline's been and gone, and that's it. Storey Racing can keep her going until December, and if British Cycling take her back that would be great. If not, there's suddenly a bit of a hole.

To keep afloat, she signs up for an agency that arranges student support for universities in the Manchester area. The plan is to get some note-taking work – it's something she's good at, and there's potentially a lot of it around – but at the start, what they need is more practical. She helps a student with autism navigate round his university. She helps another get her wheelchair out of her car. Bits and bobs, zero hours stuff at a tenner a pop.

In amongst this, she'll have to do something about a new coach, too. She's on good terms with John Hampshire and she's finding it hard to articulate exactly why she needs a change, but it just feels like something's not quite working. So it's the end of the road for the two of them for now; and she doesn't have a plan for who to go to next until it strikes her that Sarah Storey's coach, Gary Brickley, is a physiologist and an academic who has coached Paralympic trike medallist David Stone, and so it's an obvious thought to approach him.

And he agrees. They'll do some lactate testing at his laboratory, and then he'll give Hannah a four-week training protocol based on that, and they'll work from there in the hope that between them they can keep on moulding Hannah into the endurance athlete that naturally, physiologically, she really kind of isn't. Then if she doesn't improve in performance, at least they'll know exactly where they've come from and what her limits are. That's the aim, at least.

What they come up with, as a starting point, is ten to twelve hours a week – three in the gym, maybe one or two RaceRunning, and the rest on the bike. Hannah's had a discussion with Janice Eaglesham, her RaceRunning coach, and Janice is happy for her to do whatever she wants to build strength and endurance; so she's doing a bit of RaceRunning to keep her hand in the game – and to keep those muscles going – but it's not about trying to improve her performance at this stage.

Meanwhile, on the bike, they want to move her twenty minute power from where it's at right now and increase it up to just before the point where her body's capacity to deal with the lactate levels conks out. Right now, Hannah's "severe" intensity point – the bit just before you actually keel over – is kicking in at 155 watts, and she can properly give it some at around 130, but Gary wants to move the needle so she only finds it severe when she's at 180. So the sessions will go high lactate, then a rest day, followed by another lactate session, and then two endurance sessions at the weekend, and then easy, lactate, easy, lactate, and then weekend endurance all over again.

There are, at least, different types of lactate session. Right now, Fridays are a maximal, all-out, twenty minute effort, while Tuesdays are an under-over session, which is going higher than your threshold, say for five minutes, and then carrying on at just under your threshold and treating that as your "rest". It's pretty intense – and it seems to work. Gary's set some huge power targets, and Hannah's gently suggested that perhaps nobody can increase their twenty minute powers by ten watts in a week, and he's said fine and dialled it back; but while she hasn't been hitting those targets, she's been improving at an unprecedented rate. So that's good.

And Mike Ellis and Charles McCulloch are back in the picture, and they want to work with Craig Collis-McCann and David Stone as well. So Hannah's out on the road again, pounding out the hours, in the Manchester cold and the very, very wet.

She never hears back from British Cycling.

*

FOUR WOMEN IN A BOAT

In a few months' time, on an early 2018–19 season British Rowing training camp in Majorca, the coaching staff are going to take everyone aside and ask them what they think their prospects are of making it to Tokyo, and to talk about their aspirations, and Jess is going to say that she's aiming for gold.

It's great to have that sort of confidence, that if everything comes together and you can stay a bit fitter than you have been, you can win a gold medal at the Olympics. If Jess is right, though, then things will have to have gone a fuck of a lot better than they did out in Plovdiv.

Varese, the usual pre-world championships camp. Fine. The crew consolidates its progress from France a few weeks earlier and ends up top of the percentage gold medal time tables again, so in that sense, things are looking good.

But.

But Mathilda's still managing a wrist problem that she's had for most of the season, while Melissa is becoming increasingly concerned about the limited time that they've all had in the boat together. She's never felt in a position to raise things that she thinks might need changing, or at least discussing, though, because ever since she joined the crew, there's always been something just round the corner – it's the second world cup and it's our first time racing together, or it's Henley, on home water, and everybody's going to be there. Or it's the Europeans, and that's on home water again; and then oh, now it's the worlds. So she's twitchy, seeing some of the things that have been going on and wanting to say look, this isn't really how we should be behaving if we want to be winning medals. And on top of all of that, Jess knows they've not been training consistently, and that that's partly down to her, because she's still not listening to her body enough, and trying to keep going through illness and injury.

With all of which bubbling away, it's not much of a surprise that the heat feels awful, with the boat nowhere near a rhythm – even if the result, with the GB boat coming in second to Germany, looks like nothing to be too concerned about. And the semi-final is better. It feels like they're working in the same direction in training, and come race day, despite another slow start, they pick their way up the field, go from fourth to third to second. It's not all they're capable of, but it's fine.

And then, in the space of 48 hours, it all starts to fall apart. "We'd had a really solid performance in our semi," says Melissa. "We needed to be really clear about what had made that good, and absolutely insist on holding on to that. Then we maybe could have added one new thing, or turned up the intensity in one area. But instead, it felt like we just kind of chucked the race plan out of the window, and gave Mathilda a whole host of new calls to make."

It's the night before the final, and Thommo is getting wound up. He's urging them to go harder, harder than they've ever done – maybe he knows that they don't have enough, that they need to gamble if they're going to have a chance at a medal, or maybe that's just how he's decided to motivate. Then all of a sudden, they're talking about putting in another push at 750m into the race, on top of the one with 750 to go; and Melissa for one is thinking, hang on a minute. We've always had this thing about getting into our rhythm from the start, but that doesn't always happen. It might take a while. So if we're onto something good at 750, surely we want to just keep that going; and if we're not, then should we really be panicking this early? And so she makes a suggestion or two, tempering the proposed calls a bit.

Jess pushes back, and again that's not necessarily a problem, but then Melissa isn't hearing what Jess is saying in quite the same way that Jess means it, and to top it all off, there's a part of the meeting where Thommo's presumably trying to get the confidence going by asking the crew to describe their team mates' strengths, but they're all a bit on edge and it doesn't go quite as well as it might.

And sure enough, within the first ten strokes of the final, everything's gone to shit. They're not on their rhythm, they're not all pulling together, it's four different people rowing four different races. They're all trying their hardest, of course they are, but it's like they're trying to pull the boat forward rather than letting it flow underneath them – and if they did put in the push at 750, it makes no difference. Should they have gone earlier? Perhaps. Should they have abandoned the push, and just concentrated on getting back on rhythm? Maybe. Whatever happened, one thing that they can all see when they're watching it back afterwards is that they're never making inroads, and one by one Poland and Germany and the Netherlands and China cross the line, bip, bip, bip, bip, and Great Britain trail in a forgettable fifth.

You could, of course, slice that up a whole number of ways. It's fifth place at a world championships. Do that again in Austria next year, and this boat would be off to the Olympics, with time to improve and huge potential to do so. Thommo tells Jess, I've never seen someone miss as much training as you have[7] and still finish fifth in a worlds final. But Jess – and she's not the only one – is struggling to shake the feeling that something should have been done, that the race could have gone differently, while the tension within the boat feels like it's

---

7. British Rowing start to get concerned if someone's adherence to training score is over 60. Jess is at 270-odd.

building up so much that things are going to have to change, or else they could snap.

The Set-Up

"OUR OLYMPICS!"

*

FORWARDS...

When it comes to coaching, Gary Brickley knows what he's talking about. Before joining up with Hannah, he's worked with, among others, Sarah Storey, David Stone and Darren Kenny, and even with just those three that's 18 Paralympic cycling gold medals between them – a hell of a place, as they say, to be coming from.

As far as he's concerned, Hannah's situation is straightforward.

"I think she's totally capable. Physiologically, she's got a lot in her favour compared to some of her competitors. There's a lot of potential for growth, and it's not like she's got any decline. But I think, sometimes, she gets distracted.

"There's a lot that she could just clear out of her head. Things that don't really help her to perform the best she can. I think she probably overthinks things, worrying about getting to the next race, what races she's going to be doing and how she's going to beat a particular person. Things that you don't need to worry about. You've just got to get your training right, get your mind right, and then race well."

Simple as that, right – so how's she going to get there?

"I think her perception of going hard will need to change, and her perception of her ability to recover – and that will hopefully enable her to improve her performance. To give an example, if you're going at race pace for ten, fifteen minutes, and you're worried about keeping your cadence up, or your revs up, or maintaining a heart rate, so that your mind tells you that you need to slow down, I think that's something you need to learn to override. That's what a lot of top athletes that I work with are able to do – to dissociate from pain. But that's trainable. I don't think you need to train it with a psychologist, either – a good coach can deal with that."

So at the moment they're working in four week blocks, or thereabouts. "I like her way of looking at it," says Gary, "which is as an increase of one watt a week. That's a good way of looking at things, and if she could keep that going, it would be ideal. And it would get her completely in the ballpark of where she needs to be.

"In practice, what I'd probably expect would be a big jump over twelve weeks or so, and then a levelling off, and then another big jump – and part of the art of coaching is trying to know when to bring up the work to the right level to make sure that the athlete can cope with that. At the moment, though, I'm kind of treading carefully around her health,[1] which ultimately is going to define everything.

"But in terms of her classification, and who she's up against, I think she's completely competitive in that group, and if she gets her fitness right, she'll be right up there. Getting the consistency in her training, and getting up to the level that's needed, is important, and then of course there's racing smart, which is all about what happens on the day. But if you're not in the right state of mind, or your body hasn't been putting the training in, then you're not going to get there.

"At the moment – at least until I see her racing properly this year – I honestly don't know if she'll make Tokyo. There are a lot of hurdles in the way. But if everything went well, and she did all the training all the time – which never really happens, of course, but if she can eliminate those things that are having a negative impact, the things that get in the way, with health, with work, with life? Then yeah. She'll win a gold medal."

---

1. We'll come to that.

Cool.

*

CONCUSSION, DOUBT, AND THE C WORD

When she first started rowing, Jess wanted to do it all by herself. She came up through the juniors in a single, and more than that – it's the way she is, really. But for one reason or another, pretty much ever since she joined the senior setup at British Rowing, she's rowed in a quadruple scull. She's been in there with Tina and with Ro, and Melanie Wilson and Beth Rodford, and Alice, and Holly and Beth Bryan have been in and out, and then there's Zoë and Melissa, and for the last couple of years she's been alongside Mathilda.

And right now, she's utterly fed up with the lot of it.

"I just want to make a boat go fast and enjoy it," she says. It's late 2018 – Tokyo's not that far away. "If you ask me right now, I feel like I just want to work with one other person, in a double, and I want to make that go fast, and enjoy it. Because we do all this work in training, and then when it gets to competition we all seem to start rowing differently.

"At the moment, it just feels like I don't want to take that risk. Don't get me wrong, I know I've hardly done any training, because I'm constantly getting ill and injured. But I honestly believe that I'm learning from that. And I want to get to Tokyo, and I want to do well, and if I don't make it, I want to feel like that's my fault."

Let's see, then. For the start of the 2018–19 season, training means Majorca, and she starts the camp fit, and hitting the numbers. Then they go out on their bikes, down this long straight descent between one town and the next, and the road flattens, but everyone's probably still going a fair bit faster than they think they are. Jess goes to stretch her back, but all the weight's on her handlebars, on the front wheel, and she sees the wheel go.

She's not sure how she landed. She's got scrapes on both shoulders, so she's got to imagine that she hit her head, but she honestly couldn't say for sure. So there are concussion tests, and she thinks she's fine, but then someone's asking her who the Prime Minister is, and she's thinking... I know this one.

Is it Gordon Brown?

It doesn't go away. A couple of days later, they're all at dinner, and Zoë is talking about her boyfriend, and it's ridiculous, because Jess knows exactly who he is, but suddenly she can't remember his name either. The medical staff keep asking her if she's having any balance issues, and she's saying no – but you can say no all you like, and you can even believe it, but it's only come the last few days of camp that she can go down the stairs without feeling nervous. "You don't realise that until it's back," she says. "Because you just make up excuses in your head. 'Oh, it's the lighting.' 'These stairs all look the same.' Stuff like that."

So one way or another she stays off the bike, and training is quite light, and eventually the concussion goes, but the fall has definitely knocked her confidence, and left her re-evaluating things a bit. "I got away with it when I fell," she says. "I've fallen off horses so much that the reactions kicked in straight away, and because I relaxed I got away with it massively. But I've still lost two weeks of training, and it's just not worth it. Vicky Thornley didn't go out cycling on camp, she just trained on the static bike and the ergo, and I can see why, because as soon as I fell off I was just thinking, well, Vicky's made the right decision, hasn't she?

"I mean, I love cycling. But the thing is, we're not used to it. We're not out on our bikes a lot, because we're just rowing when we're back at Caversham. So when you go on camp, and you're constantly on your bike, your back's sore. You're not used to being in that position, and then you're suddenly doing 100-mile days, as well as ergos and weights. That's why I was stretching my back, and that's why I came off. It's not just me and Vicky, either – some of the girls don't even go on that camp. They have to stay at home, because their backs can't take it."

The problem is that as far as the coaching staff are concerned, you can put in a lot more hours on a bike than you can do on an ergo or out on the water; and probably more on the road than you can do on a static bike too, even if that's only because it takes longer to get bored. So if you're building up the endurance, what else is there? Running's not part of the programme – Jess used to run twice a week when she trained at Hollingworth, but it's just not a thing here, so while Vicky goes out on a Sunday, sometimes, and some of the men's team run in their spare time too, that's about it. So onwards, onwards. Feed some thoughts back to the coaching staff. See what happens.

No such luxury of time for Hannah, who's got a medical issue of her own – and where Jess's is the transient irritation of a concussion arising from a training option that can be eliminated simply enough, Hannah's struggling with the rather more worrying "big lump on her vulva" – which isn't going away, and which has, over quite a long time, been getting more and more painful.

She goes to see a plastic surgeon who's been recommended to her mother, and the surgeon says, well, you know, I deal with a lot of people with vulval cancer, so, yeah, I think it's that. And Hannah's thinking, ok... but can it be something else, though? Because for one thing, I think I'd probably rather not have cancer, and for another, actually, in the female cycling community, there are quite a few of us who get something like this.

"That's been quite triggering and scary," she says, "although to be honest, I haven't really stopped in the meantime. My training has been inconsistent, because I've had to go and prioritise these medical appointments, but it's actually going pretty well. In fact, I just did my best twenty minute power for 2018. It's all a bit topsy-turvy and stoppy-starty, but despite everything it's seemingly going in the right direction, so that's exciting." Which is great, of course, except that if surgery does prove necessary, that's going to keep her off the trike for a good couple of months.

These days, it's all self-imposed pressure, however, because she's no longer thinking in terms of getting back on the British Cycling programme. "I don't want to beat their targets," she says. "Their targets weren't evidence-based. As far as I'm concerned, they weren't really based on anything at all. So for now, I'm not looking to get back on programme, at least in terms of training. I function fine without British Cycling. It's a shame, of course, but I can still go to a world championships as a guest, as it were. Which means that I can focus on hitting the Paralympic qualification criteria, without having to do any extra stuff that might not actually count towards that.

"So that's what I'm doing. When the qualification criteria come out, that's going to be my aim. And also, because it's a transparent process, then if I tick all the boxes and they try not to take me, I can appeal that. Whereas I ticked all the boxes for them to get back on programme, or so I'd have thought, but they just said no – and that part of their process isn't transparent, so you can't appeal it. They told me that I'd done everything that they wanted me to do, and even said that it had been a delight having me on the team, but that won't get me anywhere.

"Of course, when it comes closer to Tokyo, in terms of qualification and being eligible to compete, I'd need to be on the squad, but they don't have to do that much in advance – they could put me on a week before if they wanted to. So that's what I'm aiming for now. I'm no longer jumping through their hoops."

Hmm.

*

CHANGE IN THE BOAT, CHANGE IN THE CAMP

After a while, they've just got to have it out.

"I've raised our crew dynamics within the sculling team," says Jess, "and I think a few people in the team felt that stuff wasn't working for them either. Zoë's gone back to sweep – and I don't know exactly why, but I think that this might be part of the reason for that too." So with 2019 season trials coming up, head coach Jürgen Grobler and performance lifestyle advisor Mel Chowns pull Jess and Mathilda aside into a meeting, and they talk things through.

"There'd been some problems between me and Mathilda for a while, and at that meeting, we put all our feelings on the table," says Jess. "Nothing was really resolved as such, but I think it was at least clear where we both stood, and why we felt the ways we did.

"And to be honest, even though it wasn't suddenly a case of 'oh, we're best friends now, let's go for a coffee' – but on the other hand, it's never really been like that – that whole process helped. So now, yes, I'm looking to come back into the quad project, even if this time it'd be more with a feeling of: this is my job. I have a job to do this year, and it's to qualify the quad for Tokyo."

But first, trials again, except that she's also trying to fit two years of her engineering course into one so that she can leave next year free, and that's wearing her down, so when something goes around the squad in mid-April, she comes down ill one Thursday morning, starts violently throwing up that night, and sure enough, she gets scratched. Not that it hugely matters this time, to be fair – with Beth and Holly still out, and Zoë heading back to sweep, the quad ends up pretty much picking itself: Jess, Melissa, Mathilda, and Mathilda's younger sister Charlotte. "So we're just starting up the project again, and seeing where it'll go," Jess says. If it goes well, great. If it doesn't, then they're a bit fucked – there'll be seat racing and re-selection, but not many other women to re-select from – so let's hope it goes well, or more smoothly, at least.

It feels like everyone is just trying to make the boat go fast, and that's it, and communication has been focused on that. They're not really socialising, but there seems to be some mutual respect; there's a sense that – even accounting for the injuries – everyone who's in the crew deserves to be there, and they're all bringing their own skills to the boat.

When it comes to the crunch, though? It's such a big year, this one. "I think the international racing trust will just have to come back race by race," says Jess. "For one thing, though, I think the environment that we're working in now will help, now Thommo's left. I feel able to just get on with my job, and not worry about the rest of the crew. So that's the approach that I'm taking – that I'm doing my job, and it's up to everyone else to do theirs."

Oh, yes – Paul Thompson, "Thommo", the head coach of the GB women's rowing team, the lead coach for the quad, part of the British Rowing furniture since 2000 in one form or another, has quit. Gone. Out. Not much notice – not for the athletes, at least – just up and off to China, where he'll be working alongside Steve Redgrave. Within the GB team, suddenly, the difference is massive and – to look at it with a brutal honesty that, given that it's Thommo, is probably appropriate – it feels like an improvement.

"The anxiety in the team has decreased," says Jess. "People are able to express themselves more, without fear. More ideas are out and being explored freely, and if something isn't working, then more people have a voice to say that. It feels like everything's there to help you – you're not scared that some-thing bad's going to happen.

"Don't get me wrong, Thommo was a strong character to have around, and he was a really good coach, even if it does feel a bit like some of the stuff that we're doing technically this year is the complete opposite of what we were working towards before.

"When I look back now to the first year of this Olympiad – and I think also this leads into why it felt like there was so much pressure on us to do well, and why we took so much on from other crew members – we went to him to say that we wanted to do the quad, and his reaction was like, 'Ok, well, you've said you want to do it, so you're going to have to make it work'. That kind of thing. And that was a bit like: oh, shit, ok.

"So then we decided, right, we want the defining feature of our quad to be our leg drive. Really direct, nothing getting in the way. And in the first year, I think we did that well – it was a bit overworked, and a bit inefficient, because we didn't really relax into the hull, but overall I think it was pretty good.

"Then in the second year, he made us really emphasise press-ing out – getting everything we could out of every single stroke – but that ended up inefficient too. It became more like, 'Hold on to the length, the back end, any way you can.'

"The problem was, we were trying to row the wrong length. We were trying to row the lengths that the Katherine Graingers did, and all the girls in the GB crews from the past. Sure, those quads did really well – but they were a completely different body shape to us. They were so much taller. We weren't capable of doing those long strokes, but our rig, our boat, our set-up was still the same as those 6'3" girls had had. I mean, we're strong, we're strong for our size, but we just don't have those levers.

"So this year, we've changed our blades. We've changed our

whole rig – my feet, for example, are 5cm away from where they were last year, and it's not like I've changed size – and we're not trying to row extremely long, we're just trying to be efficient with what we have. Like the back end, we want it pressed out, but we don't want to overwork it so we're falling into the bow. We want to press it out and still be on our feet to recover. To be in a better range."

So that's the plan, really – and if it loses something of the tried and tested, then perhaps it gains in the buy-in of the crew, as well as maybe – *maybe* – helping to avoid some of the injuries, because there's always a risk, of course, but so far this year, Jess hasn't picked up anything significant. The atmosphere seems to be helping with that, too – feeling able to manage the programme, and the calmer environment seems to be having a physical effect as much as a mental one – and it's such a relief to feel like if she does have a problem, she can speak up about it, and sort it out, or do something slightly different for a day or two. Being able to nip things in the bud, rather than thinking, "Oh shit, I should carry on. Oh shit, oh shit, I've got to carry on", and so on, and so on, until it all just blows up.

*

BACK IN THE SADDLE

Spring has very much sprung; and yet, while Hannah's recovering well from surgery, there's still no such thing as painless training. So that's quite worrying.

But here's the thing. When she was diagnosed – and it wasn't cancer, it was chronic swelling of the vulva – she wrote an article about the whole experience. She wrote about trying out for British Cycling in 2014 and finding herself staring at the skin and hair that had sloughed off in a hotel bathroom. She wrote about the advice that she'd had – that as long as you protect against infection, and wear padded shorts, and use chamois cream, and toughen up a bit, you'll be fine – and about how that was, quite simply, and hopefully you'll pardon the word choice here, bollocks. She wrote about the racing position, a "pressure cooker of pelvic rotation", and she wrote about how, at the heart of it all, the saddle industry was failing an entire gender.

Her article got picked up by the *Guardian*, and sure enough, people started to pay attention. All of a sudden, she had a string of companies sending her the saddles they'd made, and telling her that Theirs Was The One which would finally sort out the problem.

Which was very kind, but for one thing, it takes a huge amount of time to try out a lot of saddles, and for another, none of them quite did the trick until the very last, the one from Specialized, who had got in touch to say that they'd created a special saddle for women for exactly this reason, with someone – American cyclist Alison Tetrick – who'd had exactly the same surgery.

And then, even then, it isn't quite smooth sailing. Maybe we should bike fit you, they say, to make sure that you're using it to its full advantage, and Hannah says yeah, what a good idea, except that then, for one reason and another, they can't actually arrange a bike fit, and so Hannah goes out and gets her own one done at a bike fitter's down the road in Manchester, and touch wood that will work.

So how, then, is this saddle different? "That's what I'm supposed to be writing about next," Hannah says. "It's this whole big biomechanical, engineering discipline, which I'm not in touch with – and basically nobody is, because it's a really difficult topic – but what I can say is that all of the central bits are made of memory foam, so it's really flexible, really soft. It's also quite wide, though, so it helps you have contact with the sit bones, the pelvic regions, that would stick out in a skinny person when you sat down, the ones that you need a chair cover for. I didn't really believe in sit bones before – I have ample padding – but having been through this? Well, now I do. Very much so. So anyway, they use those as the point of contact, and that takes relief from the perineum. It's also a bit smaller than the standard one, with a shorter nose."

All of which does rather lead one to wonder why, in the name of everything that is holy, isn't something like this standard for female cyclists? For Hannah, there's only one answer. "It's women's sport, isn't it? Saddles have been created for men, for a male model, and then when they have been done for women, they've taken the male model and they've modified it a little bit. They haven't started with the female model. Which Specialized have done – they've started with someone who's had chronic stuff happen exactly like me, and then gone from there.

"When I was in the bike fit, actually, they put a pressure cover over the saddle, and when I finished the fit it looked like I had no pressure, anywhere. Which was a bit of a surprise. So I'm sure it's all going through my hands, and maybe that'll be a problem. But from the recovery perspective, I'm very excited about it. On the other hand, the fitters accidentally put my brakes on too hard, and I'm not sure how to get them off, so I've just been doing the static bike for now – but that should be sorted over the next day or two." And all that from one viral newspaper article, which has, for the time being, only one minor drawback.

Namely? "Now I'm vagina girl for ever."

Ah yes. Right you are.

Despite not feeling 100%, and not training at 100%, she and Gary have been building things up, and by the end of April she's ready for a race – a C1-level time trial, in Chester. She goes into it feeling pretty grumpy, because she's the only woman and so they want to race her in with the men, but then they also want to stretch the men, so the race looks like being twice Hannah's normal distance. That's way too far for Hannah, whether she was recovering from major surgery or not. So she agrees with them that she'll do her normal distance, which is fine, but it means that she picks up zip in terms of prize money, which isn't ideal given that she by definition wins the women's race; and there's a brief period where it looks like she might even be diddled out of Tokyo qualification points too.

"For a while, I thought I was going to get factored in against the guys," she says. "I mean, if I'm going to turn up and have a race against other women, and finish wherever in the field, then fine, give me fewer points. But if I'm doing it on my own, I need my full points. It turns out that it'll be fine, and I'm going to get my normal female points, but it was really stressful for a while. But once that was all sorted out, I did it, and I loved it. And I was like, I don't need anything! I just need racing to sustain me!"

And points, too, obvs.

Bit by bit, she's getting stronger, and Gary's a huge part of that. "I don't know exactly how he does it," she says, "but before I had my surgery, we'd got back to my previous best ever power, the one I'd done when I was kicked off British Cycling, and we exceeded it for twenty minutes.

"It's weird, because he'll send over a training plan, and I'll read it, and I'll be like, oh my god, that's way too hard. And then I'll go through the week, and it'll feel natural. I'll do a really hard session, and the next day I'll be thinking, I haven't got much left, I don't think I can do any more. And then I'll look at the plan, and I'll be like oh, yes, I feel like my legs want to do that long ride now. It just flows."

Of course, it's not quite the same post-surgery, but Hannah's back on the trike. The deal with Gary is very much ad hoc, so there's no "programme" that she's missing out on as such – instead, when she's ready, she'll tell him she wants some training, and then he'll give her a block and she'll tell him how it feels.

She's still going to the gym too, trying to keep up the strength work. "I was in surgery twice," she says, "and I was out the morning after and in the gym within a day both times. It's just getting back on the saddle had to wait four to six weeks.

"But because I had the surgery up in Scotland, I've not really had that much follow up. I've got a medical liaison doctor from the Scottish Institute and my surgeon on WhatsApp, though" – and yes, I'm sorry to say that this is going exactly where you think it's going – "so it's been a case of photographs. 'How does this look? Can I get back on now?'"

Eesh.

Careful with those notifications.

The timing means that she should still be able to peak during the racing season, hopefully in time for the third world cup race in Canada in August, which could in turn give her a shot at qualifying for the world championships. "The qualification criteria haven't come out, they will probably be published the day after Ostend or something, so I'm just pedalling into the dark and hoping," says Hannah. "And then, if British Cycling want to take me, they'll take me. They'll probably charge me a bucket, but yeah."

Yeah, on that. Finances, still a problem. Storey Racing have committed to paying Hannah's race costs for the season, but even that's a bit tricky, because Sarah's said that she can't give her the money in advance. No problem, right? Hannah can get a credit card and pay for things, and then Sarah can pay her back – except that she can't qualify for a halfway decent credit card, because she isn't earning enough. On the plus side, the *Guardian* article's brought in some cash, her increased profile has led to a few commissions for other articles and a speaking job or two, and she's talked her way into co-hosting a new disability sport podcast for the BBC, so that should keep the wolf from the balance book for the time being. Then all she needs to do is finish off her Master's which is almost done but isn't quite and is now overdue and then, maybe, she can concentrate on cycling again for a while.

Belgium, for a world cup. Perhaps a C1 race in Austria a few weeks later if she can get enough of a support team together, then the Cologne Classic again, then maybe another C1 over in Switzerland. At the end of June, there's a C1 in Bilbao in Spain, and then a little break in July, possibly work on her RaceRunning a bit, to see if she's still got it and could maybe qualify for the Para-Athletics World Championships in November.

LEARNING TO STEP BACK

All change. Little stuff, but lots of it, and the British Rowing women's training programme has suddenly got a completely different vibe. No longer does it feel like they're just doing the same thing, week in week out, it feels like there's a context. Sure, there are still plenty of big, heavy days, but maybe now there'll be a half day off that's thrown in before. Things like that. Everything being taken into consideration; and it comes across as thought out, rather than, well, this worked last time, let's just add in some more. "It adds up," says Jess, "and what it adds up to is being able to do all the pieces properly. To do them for what they are."

The beginnings of a taper, a focusing of effort even at this stage towards Tokyo? Possibly, but it's not being presented like that, and anyway the quad still needs to qualify, and in a tight, competitive field, that means they're going to need to hit this year's world championships – the first qualification event – in tip-top shape.

Jürgen Grobler is more visible now. He's not on the ground with them all the time – Paul Reedy and Jane Hall are leading the day-to-day sculling coaching – but he's helping to set the programme, he'll have meetings with the team sometimes, and he'll be there for a camp or two. And the team feels happier, at least as Jess sees it. "There's been a lot of seat racing," she says, "but there's not the same sense of everyone being played against each other, so it feels like selection is trusted a lot more."

In the quad, training seems to be going well, which makes the European Championships in Lucerne, which will kick off their racing season, an opportunity to put a stake in the ground. Like in 2017, like in 2018 – although perhaps for slightly different reasons now – there are plenty of reasons to think that they're nowhere near the finished article, but maybe that's fine. "We'll just see where we are and what we need to do," says Jess. "That's what the coaches are saying now. Whereas Thommo would be more like, 'Why aren't you aiming for the gold medal? You should always be aiming for a gold medal, because if you're not aiming for gold, you're not even going to get on the podium.' And I respect that approach – I was part of it – but it does create more stress, when it's not needed. Obviously when we're in a race, we're always going to be trying to go the fastest we can. I'm not going to hold back, and not push for a gold medal, just because someone's said that if we come sixth it's all right. Of course the result matters. But it got to that stage for every race – and even down to some of the lower intensity training sessions.

"Ultimately, I think it's about trust and respect. We're all athletes, we're all there for the same reason, and we've got ourselves there because we want to win. We don't need to kid ourselves. We don't need to pretend."

The new atmosphere's also putting some of their old performances into context, all the way back to their first race of the Olympiad, the Belgrade World Cup in 2017. "We didn't perform well, absolutely," says Jess. "But we felt so much pressure going into that race. I was so wound up on the start line – I can see it in my face when I watch it back – and I suspect that the reason for that is because we'd crashed twice in the warm-up just before, which was just embarrassing. We weren't doing what we usually do, and that was just because of the day-to-day pressure.

"And then that performance went down so badly. I'd just won my first senior medal, but the sense, straightaway, was no, I hadn't won it, I'd come last. Even going up to the medal pontoon felt crushing. And of course I'd come last, I know as an athlete that I'd come last, but I was so unhappy.

"It was awful. There was one meeting after that, that was put in to talk about that result, and I had a panic attack. I couldn't breathe, I had to leave the room. Whereas if that race were to happen now, the whole atmosphere would be much more positive. 'Let's see what we can do, this is exciting, we're a brand new project, we're racing Olympic medallists', that sort of thing. It could have been so different."

There's a bigger issue here, of course.

Or rather, there are several bigger issues. Issues with big and important names such as Elite Performance Mentality and Ethics and The Psychology of the Individual and Funding and National Responsibility, all of which bubble away and boil down to: what, exactly, is all of this for? And once that's been decided – and good luck with that – who is the best person to be in charge and try to make that happen? For the GB women's squad, it's been Paul Thompson, it's now Jürgen Grobler, and when it was Paul, there was a lot of this sort of attitude going around – and you know what? Some of it, for some people, was probably exactly what they needed.

For Jess, then? Was that experience, the only one that she has ever known at this level, the making of her? Did it toughen her up? Is she a stronger character for going through it all? "Yeah. I definitely feel like I am." Cool. "But also," – oh no wait, hang on – "I think too much so. So that's why I'm trying to learn to step back a bit. Just do my job. That's my responsibility. Other people's actions aren't my responsibility.

"But at least I don't feel scared about approaching people now. And I've definitely learnt a lot about how to work around people's different personalities, and about holding myself to a certain standard in every single session."

It's madly complicated, and it's difficult not to feel some sympathy for the Thompson approach, but for the sake of clear-headedness we're going to tell nuance to do one, because, well, Jess is happier now, and it's hard to see that as a bad thing. "I definitely feel like I'm more likely to carry on rowing after Tokyo, to be honest. It's not like I had a serious wobble about this Olympiad, but there was definitely a point where I was like, oh my god, do I really want to carry on doing this for another four years? But now, at least, I'm enjoying it more."

And so to the Europeans, which will see Jess at bow, Melissa at two, Mathilda at three and Charlotte at stroke. They're getting towards the rhythm they're after, the picture that the coaches have in their minds of what it should look like, and if the Europeans go well, they'll stick to it. There's been a rejig of calling – Melissa will do the calls based on the race plan, and Jess herself will cover the more on-the-run stuff, the responsive side. They've spoken to the team's new sports psychologist, and run through an exercise that involves talking about what they're going to hear, what they're going to do, what they see happening when they're racing their best race and when people are doing their best training, things like that. The crew and the coaches have set out their personal priorities, too – for instance, Mathilda's is about opening discussions, while Charlotte's is about delivering the best possible rhythm from her position at stroke.

And Jess? For her, it's exactly what she's been saying to herself – about doing her share, her 25 per cent. Trying, for the first time in a long time, not to worry about other people.

*

AND YET, AND YET

There's a new rider at Ostend.

The second world cup race of 2019 should really be about Hannah's triumphant return from surgery to pick up her first ever world medal, but as far as she's concerned, what with one thing and another – well, no, with one thing in particular – it's not. It's about the new rider.

She's called Angelika. She's 50-something, she looks to be in similar physical shape to Monica Sereda, she finishes a fair whack behind Hannah in the time trial before blowing her away in the road race, and until fairly recently, she could ride on two wheels.

"If I'm honest, I've lost a bit of faith in the classification system," says Hannah. "Because to me, it looks like they're letting in someone who's already got a race.

"I mean, it's not really about being at the top of the classification or not. She's already got a race as a C4 – and fine, maybe she wasn't really a C4, but if not, then she could be moved to C3. As far as I can tell, she has no problem cornering, no problem with her pedal stroke, no adaptations – and if she can ride a two-wheeled bike, it seems to me that there's no reason why she should be a trike."

When it comes down to it, though, there's not much that Hannah can do. She mentions her concerns to British Cycling, in case they think there's anything that could be taken further, but once she's done that, she's going to try not to think about it any more. Control the controllables – like applying for the world championships.

British Cycling haven't given Hannah much notice about how and when to apply – in fact, they don't even tell her directly, she finds out via Storey Racing team mate Katie Toft

– and then it's really hard to find the form. But she tracks it down, fills it in, and because as luck would have it there's only one competition that they're going to take into account and it's the one at which she's just won a bronze, off she's going to go. Not only that, indeed, but this year, they're not going to charge her for the privilege. So there's a thing.

She's still planning to race at the world cup in Canada – not least because the Storeys will be covering her costs, and Scottish Cycling are paying for someone to go and support her – but she won't have to prove anything. It'll be a chance to hopefully show some form, win some Tokyo qualification points, and just do a bit more racing.

Because the plan had been to travel around Europe, race a few C1s, pick up some points, but then the person who was going to come and support her while she did that had a car (good), but a car that couldn't fit Hannah or her trike in it (less good). Hannah had been so focused on Belgium, she'd left herself to sort out the C1s afterwards; and she'd lined up her support, but in a "Hey, are you going to be there, cool, we'll do our thing" kind of a way.

No dice.

"It looks like what I have to do is continue to be this ruthless micro-manager of people," she says. "Sometimes, especially when I'm knackered, I switch off on that." At least she's going to all the world competitions she can for the rest of the season, though, with Canada and the world championships. Add in the Chester C1, and there's going to be a C1 in Harrogate at the tail end of the season too – the Yorkshire 2019 Para-Cycling International, no less – and maybe that's about as much as she would physically be capable of anyway. Sarah's pretty confident that Great Britain will still be top of the points table for Tokyo qualification in any event, but as Hannah points out, "You never want to be complacent, because if it turns out that they couldn't quite get enough points to send seven women, and they can only send six, then maybe that's me who loses out, you know?" Luckily Katie Toft, for one, is off competing all over the place and winning everything, so that will help.

And the days are warm and sunny. She pops back up to Glasgow for a bit, and Glasgow has a lot fewer cars than Manchester, so training feels smooth and super speedy. They haven't been tracking powers recently, they've not done tests, with Hannah still on her way back from surgery, but training blocks are getting longer, and she's making gains in the gym. Strongest ever squat sets, intense five minute efforts, that sort of thing. The saddle's not exactly fixed, but it's not giving her as much pain – the swelling reappears after long rides but then goes down again, and she's building in recovery days to try to keep it under control.

And yet, and yet. The day that Hannah hears that she's been selected for the world championships, she'd been close to tears, telling Sarah that she doesn't think that she can do this, and how she doesn't feel like there's anything tying her to cycling. She's emailed Jon Pett, head of para-cycling at British Cycling, to say that she needs to know if they're going to take her on programme or not – logistical stuff, like is she going to have to heat train, and what might or might not she have access to before the Paralympics – and there's been nothing back. Most of the time, something like that is fine – carry on regardless, don't really think about it, and it's nothing.

On the bad days, though, it can feel like everything.

It means that she'll probably need to get a job again in the winter season, and little things like when something goes wrong on her trike, she'll have to find the money for a mechanic. It just makes everything that little bit harder.

BEATING THE DUTCH

Lucerne.

The European Championships – the event where the Great Britain quad made its breakthrough, a couple of years back. This year, though, they're not making an impression. Second in the heat, third in the repêchage, a distant fifth place in the final.

Could they have expected much more, with what they had? It's Charlotte's first race in the senior quad, and Mathilda's only just finished the final exams for her degree, so she hasn't really been training and is really quite unfit. "I think we kind of put a rhythm down, which was a positive," says Jess, "but it wasn't a rhythm that we would actually want to row." Oh. "Basically, we navigated ourselves through three races together."

Through their new personal relationships, too. Everything between Jess and Mathilda still feels a bit raw, but there are no flare-ups. They even end up sharing a room – which doesn't seem to be a deliberate effort on the part of the coaching staff to bring them together and break through their differences, but rather a logistical coincidence – and as it happens, it's fine. At the end of the regatta, they talk about it all, and it feels like the start of something again.

There's one thing in particular that probably helps, in fact. First thing when they get to the hotel, off they go to their room, but they haven't quite picked up where they need to be next, and when they need to be there. So Mathilda gets her laptop out, and Jess has a little lie down, and suddenly there's a phone call to the room – "Where are you? Where are you?" – and they've both fallen asleep, Mathilda while still sitting up, and it's all a bit of a panic to get their stuff together and get themselves onto the bus to the course. Which rather breaks the ice.

There had been a suggestion that the quad would race again at the season's second world cup, in Poznań, but Jürgen decides that they need more time together to work up a bit more speed, and that the best way to do that is to go back to a solid training block and get some good base work done, rather than just going to another race and probably putting in a similar performance. Take a step back, build up, invest some time in understanding that rhythm that Jess was talking about, and then try to put together a full race at Henley. Jess wants to experiment with the order, just to see how it could work, and if people might work better in different seats. "We haven't done it with this crew, so why not give it a chance? While we've got a big training block." But the decision's made not to, and so be it. They're happy with how everyone's suited to their jobs.

So onwards to Henley, and it feels like there's a bit of a change in the air. To some of the others around the squad, it seems like Jess is letting a bit more of her personality out around race time; and when she thinks about it, maybe she did feel like she had to dampen down some of herself when she was working under Paul Thompson. Either way, it's going down really well with everyone that she's just getting excited about racing.

And with good reason, too. The first race goes by, fairly uneventful, a two and a quarter length win against Amsterdamsche Studenten Roeivereeniging Nereus and Koninklijke Studenten Roeivereeniging Njord,[2] and then in the semi-final, suddenly they're up against the Netherlands senior boat – and not only that, but it's also a full-strength Dutch line-up. It's the visitors who start better, despite clipping a duck on their way up the river – and there's the best part of a length between the

2. Try saying that after a night out in Henley.

boats by halfway, but the British won't go away, and they keep coming back, and coming back, and pushing all the way to the line, and even if they end up missing out on a place in the final by little more than a nostril hair, these two boats have never been that close. "We had a really good race," says Jess. "We were a real team, and we fought. We really fought for it, we were brave, we attacked early."

The early attack feels like an important milestone. It's a reactive one – Jess senses that they have to go for it, so that's what she calls, and everyone responds. They're trusting her to make the right call, and they do exactly what she's asking of them, putting their bodies on the line – and for the first time in a while, they've really changed the dynamics of a race on the water. So sure, it's a defeat, but there's a feeling in the boat that they've done something special.

That helps Jess on a personal level, too. Maybe there's a hint of pride – "I called that" – but it doesn't really matter what name you give it. She's excited, she's attacked the race, it's been more ferocious, a bit less clinical. She's raced how she wanted to, and she's been backed up with positive feedback from the team as well.

All told, it's a massive boost, which they carry forward into the third world cup in Rotterdam – where they beat the Dutch again, twice, and on home water.

There are eight boats in the field, which means a full complement of heat, repêchage and final; and they're all pretty good performances for the British quad. For one thing, the starts are positive – they're staying with the pack at least, which they haven't really managed to do all Olympiad. There's no particular change that they can pin that on, although it does seem like one of Charlotte's strengths is setting and pulling her crew mates along to a nice high rate.

It adds up to fourth place in the final, behind Germany,

Poland and the Australians, but ahead of a pretty much full-strength Netherlands, who they'd beaten in the rep as well – and that feels all the better given that pretty much on arrival at the regatta, Jess came down with something which, on a normal day, would have laid her out. "If we hadn't been racing, I probably wouldn't have got out of bed," she says. "I think the girls knew I wasn't in a very good state, and so they were just helping, doing whatever they could, and I was doing whatever I could, and that was about it. We did well, but that was definitely in spite of having me on board."

And that's it, the final regatta before the world championships. The last race before Linz, at which the top eight boats – so the A finalists and the top two in the B final – will qualify for Tokyo.

So off to Varese – two and half weeks at first, back home for a couple of days to do a spot of washing and sleep in your own bed for a bit, then back out again. And it's a solid chunk of hard work, and everyone's really consistent, and they're having a really good time. They're going through everything – technical models, communication, weights work, team dynamics – and they're going really fast.

They're coming top of percentage gold medal time, which feels like a positive, although they've been in similar positions before over the Olympiad, and it hasn't always translated into race performances. That doesn't hugely fuss Jess for the moment, though – "We're just trying to do our best, and the percentage gold medal times are what come out of that" – and she's getting further confidence from something that they've been calling "Project 6:10". It's not exactly complicated – it's just about being able to cover a 2k run in 6 minutes 10 seconds, because they reckon that'd probably be quite a good time to be able to do, and they've never gone that fast before, in training or at a race – and by the end of the camp, they've done it.

Of course, this isn't Jess's first Olympiad, so she knows that however well they're doing now, there'll be completely different circumstances and pressures in Linz, but the difference from the last few years is that they're not being asked to perform magic this time. Just go out, do what you've been doing, and that's all we can really ask. If there's some magic there, it'll come, but if not, you're doing fine.

Don't worry about what happened last time.

*

JANICE

Hannah doesn't go to Canada.

He was just a kid, Gavin, knee-high to a grasshopper, but he'd been absolutely gunning it on his running bike, so he'd come along to the club, to Red Star Athletics in the east end of Glasgow, with its army of enthusiastic amateurs of all ages and abilities, and Janice Eaglesham had taken him under her wing. For free, because she felt that it was important.

He'd started to get good, and a while later, Kayleigh Haggo had joined the club and she'd been good too, and so Janice had taken them both to some international competitions, and then a little while after that, along came a 19-year-old Hannah.

A really unfit, overweight, first year of university, been-on-a-RaceRunner-once Hannah – who'd realised that she wanted to do sport, but wasn't getting anywhere with the university. She didn't think of herself as a potential elite athlete then, but she wanted to get good. She didn't just want to run recreationally, she wanted to go fast. To make an impression.

"That's no problem," said Janice. "How much do you want to train?"

So with a RaceRunner and a piece of paper, off they went, six days a week. "I came back to race six months later," Hannah says, "and I'd made so much progress, and she was so enthusiastic, that I just fell in love with sport. Janice and Gavin – they taught me what sport was."

Because sport – as Hannah has learnt since – is not nice, it's about money and medals; but like with Gavin, Janice never asked Hannah for a penny. No social media promotion, nothing. "All she wanted for me and Gavin and Kayleigh was that we would have fun on our RaceRunners, and that we would achieve what we wanted to achieve. She spent hours with us, literally hours and hours – and why would anyone do that? Why would anyone spend so much time?

"And through all of it, she was never moody, and she never lost belief. She pushed us, but she'd always have faith." And in due course, there came a time when Janice said right, Hannah, you're ready to compete. In fact, you know what, I think you'll be one of the fastest in the world.

One thing, of course, led to another, and another, and another, and to Rio, but throughout it all, Janice totally understood. There was never any pressure to keep going with the RaceRunning, but she'd be there if Hannah needed her – for a chat, a coffee, a how are you.

So they made a plan, and they didn't really tell anybody about it, but it all started to come together as RaceRunning was edging closer and closer to the mainstream, and the plan was that once Tokyo was over, they were all going to work together towards Paris 2024, Hannah and Janice, Gavin and Kayleigh – like they had at the 2018 Para-Athletics Worlds, days and days of training, full on, goodness knows how Janice made ends meet kind of stuff.

"I was always anxious," Hannah says. "I wish I was the kind of person, like Janice and Ian, that could spend two nights a week herding these crazy people around a track, trying to organise everything and do everything, and be invested in everyone. But I just couldn't. So I was so anxious that they were going to retire. Because for me, they're the true meaning of sport – about investing in athletes fully, and seeing them through to their events, and believing in them. Facilitating, removing every barrier to ensure that they can enjoy what they're doing. Because that's just not what I've experienced anywhere else – it's always like, you have to jump through this hoop.

"Since I've been off the British Cycling programme, it's become really hard, doing everything I do and maintaining what I believe is the life of an elite athlete. And Janice just knew – at the crunch points, like with my surgery, she'd know that I was struggling, more than I'd ever done, and she would just phone me up and we'd have a chat. She didn't have those boundaries that other coaches do. I always felt that she cared about me, regardless of whether or not I wanted to do RaceRunning. She would ask me sometimes, which do you love more?, and I was like, of course I love RaceRunning more! And you know what, I think I do, and it's mostly because of Janice.

"For her, sport was about having fun. I don't believe in racing if you're not going to race for a personal best – it's a waste of a race, whatever the colour of the medal. But Janice would always be like, no, just race to have fun. Race because you love it. Race because you want to treat it with respect. Be brilliant because it's such a beautiful sport to do, and you're giving your everything and showing it off – and I always used to say, yeah, but it's about victory as well, you know? Beating other athletes…"

In the autumn of 2019, Janice was training towards a triathlon, to raise money for the RaceRunners in Red Star – and she was going to use some of the money to make up some t-shirts, which would say "RaceRunners Run for Fun" on the back. Well, said Hannah, on the front, I want "RaceRunners Run for Blood and Glory", or something like that.

And while she was training, she crashed and broke her arm; and she went back to training, and back to coaching, and she was fine, and she got the cast off, and then she had a blood clot, and she had a stroke, and suddenly, she was gone.

"What can we do? The world didn't end – but I needed for it to end for a bit, for me. I needed, just for a while, not to carry on. It's interesting how people perceive mental strength in sport, isn't it? I think it would have been doing her a disservice.

"I missed my competition in Canada. I think that has destabilised a lot of other relationships in my life, with Storey Racing, with Scottish Cycling, because in so much of sport, people operate on what you can give back to them. I think both of them were understanding at the time, and I was able, without much faff, to go within myself and grieve, but I still think people don't understand it. And that's for them not to understand, but... yeah."

*

SO FAR AWAY

The Para-Cycling World Championships, Emmen, September 2019. Not long to go.

Something has changed.

And it's not good.

Hannah's been training fine – surgery be damned, she's putting up the best powers that she's ever done. Then along comes the time trial, and she's seven minutes back from the podium.

It's never felt so far away. "It's just rubbish," she says. "In the end, I was pushing myself so hard that I crashed. And I'm just like, are you kidding me?"

So many competitors that – as far as Hannah's concerned – are nigh on able-bodied. There's even a new T1 who looks like she could go faster than Hannah.

"I really feel like I'm seeing the difference in ability with some of the T2s now. I can't corner like they can, I can't come off the saddle – it's really significantly different from my disability. And I'm the only person there who has more than one limb impaired in my class. So in terms of performance, it wasn't a very good world championships – but what it did do was say to me that maybe I need to try to get my classification reviewed."

So once she gets back from the Netherlands, that's what she's doing. She takes soundings from someone who works in athletics classification, who examines Hannah and reviews the criteria and tells Hannah that as far as she's concerned, Hannah's got grade three spasticity in both of her legs. Which would make her a pretty good fit for T1, and takes away one worry that Hannah's been having – am I just, she's been thinking, being an idiot?

It's going to be complicated. She'll need to get a fair amount of medical evidence together, because normally, to get your classification reviewed, your disability needs to have changed, and Hannah doesn't think that that's what's happened here. The hope – and Hannah's perception – is that the system's understanding of neurological disabilities has evolved; but either way, there's a full process that has to be gone through. She'll have to get herself assessed, pass her up-to-date medical documentation onto British Cycling – "Hannah has cerebral palsy, this is the impairment she has, this is the doctor who's said that and who's tested her" – and then hopefully they'll agree that it looks like she might be a T1. Then the classifiers will come and watch her, and see what they think.

Things could have changed. It might be that Hannah has deteriorated physiologically, and just hasn't admitted that to herself. Maybe something related to her saddle injury – it's caused huge amounts of muscle strain and motor function pain, so maybe it's made her legs more spastic? Because the difference between T1 and T2 is one grade of perceived muscle spasticity, and Hannah is getting older – as one does – and that can lead to a decline in function for people with cerebral palsy, so maybe when the surgeons and the classifiers look at her, they'll see some difference.

And all of that, and for why?

It starts, really, right at the beginning of the Olympiad. She's been picking up fourths and fifths for a couple of years, but that's because she's been on that "ski jump to Rio" that her coach talked about, and now she's going to do things properly. Fine, she's thinking – I'm starting out, I train up, and then, eventually, the gap closes. Except that she doesn't believe that any more, because injuries, context, on-programme, off-programme, whatever, this is a young athlete who's been training at a high level for a long time, and it feels like she's getting

absolutely nowhere. "I am strong," she says. "I am an elite athlete. And the gap has just got bigger. So I need to push for
change now."

Yes, it's about winning a medal. Of course it is. Of course
Hannah would prefer to have a race where she has a better
chance of making an impact. Of course she doesn't want to
be seven minutes back from the podium in a time trial, and of
course, if she gets reclassified into T1, that'll bump her up the
standings and might even push her straight into contention for
gold. But it's more than that. It's about the future of the sport.

"There are a few girls who have had similar disabilities to
mine," she says, "and they've been seven minutes, ten minutes,
fifteen minutes back. They're my age, they're my disability,
and they weren't competitive at all, so they've just quit. Say I
don't go to Tokyo, and that ends up being it, what would I like
to leave as a legacy? I'd like to be able to look someone at the
UCI in the eye and ask them, do you want to see girls quitting? Because they're going to. And the reason they're going
to is because of classification."

In the meantime, though, while that all bubbles away, there's
Harrogate a week later for the Yorkshire 2019 Para-Cycling
International – which sounds fantastic, but they really don't
seem to have thought it through. "They didn't have anybody
on a hand bike or a trike recce it, as far as I know, so while
they've picked a shorter route, it's hugely hilly and very technical. It's completely impossible for trikes," says Hannah.

"Unfortunately, though, I had to be a spokesperson for it, so
I'm just going to be there to look happy and pretend to be a
good disabled person doing an integrated race. But that's about
it. Sleep over on the Friday, race on the Saturday afternoon,
drive straight back to Manchester."

Sure enough, it doesn't go well. Hannah has spasms throughout the race such as she's never had before – not in a race, anyway – and the whole thing is way too challenging. "I actually had to stop during the race – several times – because I was in so much pain," she says. "Nobody was with me, and it was terrible. I was in agony, and by the time it got to three kilometres from the finish I was like, I'm not sure I can make it round. I felt ridiculous, very melodramatic, but I couldn't stay on my trike, and my legs were seizing up. In the end, the driver of the race ambulance got on a motorbike, and just drove with me for the last three kilometres.

"I was so fatigued from the world championships, and it feels like I've crashed more times in the last couple of months than I ever have before, and it just made me think – you know what? I'm not sure I want to do this any more."

So she takes some time out – three weeks, completely away from cycling, because she needs to find out whether she still really wants this.

*

LINZ

New Zealand, China, Australia, Great Britain, Russia, France. For the winner, it's straight through to the A final and Tokyo; for everyone else, it'll be the repêchage.

China are the stand-outs. They've been performing all year – gold in Plovdiv at World Cup I, gold in Poznań at World Cup II, before giving Rotterdam a miss – and they came fourth at the 2018 World Championships too, and perhaps should have done better.

The announcer does the final call-out, the lights flip, and that's the last time it's a level field. Barely a minute gone, not even 500m through, and the Chinese are the best part of 20 metres ahead, clear water between them and Great Britain in second.

Second 500 and the gap's getting wider if anything, so the British boat falls back on the pre-race plan, which is that if they're not going to win it, they're going to conserve some energy. Jess gives out a call or two here, a bit of leaving them to it there, keep things ticking over.

New Zealand are tracking with Great Britain, which is something of a surprise, and Australia aren't, which is even more so. Obviously with China so far out in front and the only A final place sewn up, it's difficult to gauge the effort that everyone else is putting in, but it's only the Kiwis and the British who are looking halfway competitive.

With a bit of hindsight, the crew should probably have talked about what would be their best route through the regatta. Second place goes into one repêchage, third into the other, and so on, and so perhaps if they'd put in a bit of a push and got their noses ahead of New Zealand at the line, they'd not have ended up on the tougher side of the draw, and in a scrap with Poland and the USA for the next two qualification spots.

But that's very much where they are – Great Britain, Poland and the Americans alongside Romania, the Aussies and France, with two places up for grabs in the A final, and with that, in Tokyo. Which plays on the mind a bit in the days between the heat and the repêchage: if the heat was something of a free swing – give it what you can to start with, but if the Chinese do what's expected of them, then don't keep pushing – this is a bit more of a big deal.

Not, however – and this makes a pleasant change, for a world championships – that that's coming through in the atmosphere around the camp. Not for this year a bust-up over when someone is supposed to be on a bus. Not for this year the lingering doubt about whether everyone in the boat is pulling in the same direction. Have a good time, chill, just treat it like any other race, go about your daily business, don't think too much about being 48 hours away from the Olympics.

Off go Poland. Not a big surprise, given how consistent they've been over the past few years. They're in the repêchage because they got pipped by the Dutch in their heat, but like it's been since the start of the Olympiad, it's Kobus-Zawojska at bow, Wieliczko at 2, Springwald at 3, Zillmann at stroke, and like they have since the start of the Olympiad, they're looking strong. The British crew have tried not to spend much time wondering about what to expect from other boats – keep it internal, just work on getting from A to B as fast as we can – so while they've been talking about trying to get into the race a bit more off the start, they're not going to change their race plans because of any other crew in particular.

So off go Poland. Out they step in front of the field, and they're looking comfortable enough. Five hundred metres in, and Great Britain are in third, which is fine, and they're more than in touch with the Americans, but it's still third, which will mean a B final where only the top two will be going to the Olympics, and where the pressure is going to be immense.

It's Jess's job to make the in-race calls, and it can be tricky in a position like this – push now, and will you have something left at the end? Push later, and risk giving yourself too much to do? The 500 into the 1k, and she's holding her nerve.

Into the 1k, half the race gone, and Jess looks over, and whoa, hang on, they've got half a length on us now.

She's been to that wash-up regatta they have in Olympic year. She was there in 2016, when she, and Ro, and Tina, and Holly finished five seconds short of Rio.

She's come last in the rain in Belgrade, and she's seen two of the crew that sat in that boat lose some of their best years to injury.

She's seen an Olympic medallist come in to the project, give it a year and then head straight back out again, and there've been times when she wanted out of the boat herself.

She's been through panic attacks, and rib injuries, and she's catapulted herself over her handlebars.

But in front of her are Charlotte, and Mathilda, and Melissa, and they don't know what's going on around them, but they're listening, and waiting, and she knows that they're going to do what they tell her.

She's not panicking. Or, at least, she's doing her best not to *sound* panicked, which is tricky given how she knows that this, right now, is the moment. This is the moment when they have to attack, when they have to go, because otherwise this is the moment when it could all just slip away.

And she calls for an attack. And they go.

And it's not enough.

Not yet.

They've edged into second with 500 metres to go, but it's impossibly close, so they're going to have to attack again. Oh fuck, here come the Americans. Here they come.

And there's only one call.

Every bit of energy that Jess can spare.

"OUR OLYMPICS!"

400 metres. 300 metres. 200, and with every stroke, the American boat is closing.

"OUR OLYMPICS!"

To the line.

B-beep.

Two boats, eight women. One place on the plane.

Jess is vaguely aware that Jane, the coach, is screaming. Is this a good scream? Is it a bad scream? Does she even know yet?

And in the end, it's Mathilda. Given everything that's gone on between them, all the difficulties, all the question marks, all the history, of course it's Mathilda.

"We've qualified."

No, no, no. No we haven't.

"It's on the board."

They've done it. By 0.2 seconds, they've done it. And right now, Jess is probably swearing a lot, and crying a lot, and thanking everyone in the boat, and hugging them. But she can't, in all honesty, remember a moment of it.

Still a race to go, after all of that. There's an afternoon of enjoying the feeling, living the emotion of qualifying, but they're not even going as far as a sip of champagne before it's back on the horse for the A final.

Where they finish last – albeit not by much behind Germany and New Zealand. The medals go to China – in front wire to wire, not nearly for the first time and quite probably not for the last – who are followed home by Poland and the Netherlands, and all three are going to be hard to beat come Tokyo; but – and sure, stop us if you've heard this before – it doesn't feel like a perfect reflection of where things are, or where they might yet be. Four days ago, this patched-up British quad, with one sculler who's in her first senior season, and another who was at university a couple of years back, put in the race of their lives – so for all that they're giving it some in this final, some is pretty much all they've got left. And as for next year? There's a world championships medallist – maybe two – who'll be pushing to get back in.

But for now, it is what it is. And there's a good party on the night of the final, out in Linz. The day after, though, Jess just stays in, because the day after that, she'll be going on a road trip through France with Adam, her boyfriend; and she may be a prospective Olympian now, but even prospective Olympians don't enjoy being hungover in a van.

*

SCOTTIE

Three weeks.

Surfing, to start. An impromptu drive down to Cornwall – see it, book it, do it. Adapted surfing, and only the one session, but it's beautiful. The board is basically a rescue board, with little handles, because Hannah can't really swim in open water – her body doesn't know which way is up, so she can't right herself – and so she lies down on it, catches a few waves, and it's a positive experience of the sea for what feels like the first time in her life.

Then back up to the Lake District, for an adventure camp. It's been in the diary for a while, this one, this week or so of canoeing and sailing and high-wires and fire building and something called "The Drop" which is exactly what it sounds like – for people with cerebral palsy who missed out on stuff like this when they were younger, and there wasn't such a push to be active.

But none of it – no, not even The Drop – is quite like cycling. There are all sorts of reasons why Hannah should enjoy it, and so many reasons why she does – it's giving her the adrenaline rush that she lives for, the thrill, the fun, the team spirit – but there's nothing that brings her that joy. There's nothing that takes her so far.

So that settles it, really. For the next nine months or so, it's going to be cycling. It's going to be cycling all the way.

Without Gary, though, which is a shame. He's been brilliant – "I've never had such good training from a coach" – and Hannah's asked him if he wants to stick around, but she's also said that she appreciates that last season was difficult for one reason or another, so she'll understand if he doesn't want to; and that's pretty much where they leave it.

Then one evening soon after that, she's sharing a pizza with Helen Scott – "Scottie" – a multiple world and Paralympic gold medal-winning cyclist to whom she's grown so close that it's entirely possible that the room at Hannah's place in which they're eating also contains a cushion with a picture of Scottie's face on it (a birthday present from the latter); and she's thinking out loud about what to do given how little time there is left before Tokyo, and Helen says, you know, Han, why don't I give you a hand? After all, I know you really well, I owe you for all that physiology tutoring you gave me a couple of years back, *and* I've been coaching riders for ten years now – so how about I set the training? I'll push you out of your comfort zone, we'll make sure we're hitting all the right zones and stuff, and I'll be the point of security for you, someone to keep you accountable. So that's what they'll do.

Mike and Charles are still bobbing around too. They came to the world championships, they came to Harrogate, and Hannah's getting along with them really well at the moment. They were the ones who helped her get back on the road after Janice died, when Hannah was having difficulty getting back into it because of the guilt that she was feeling about not spending the time with Janice that she could have done. It was Mike and Charles who looked after her then, and took her out cycling – albeit on a really challenging part of the Goyt Valley in the Peak District, and a particularly steep hill that was the first in her long line of crashes.

They might be getting to the bottom of that now, at least. In between another fitting and switching over to her winter training trike, it's become clear that the change of position that Hannah has made in order to alleviate the pressure on her saddle might feel a lot better on the bum, but has pushed her way too far forward onto the handlebars, which in turn has made her much less stable, and much more likely to crash.

"I'm trying to work it out," she says, "and I can't, really, but I'm just going on the road anyway.

"Fuck it, you know?"

So over winter, Helen's going to set out some templates and put together some sessions, and every now and again Hannah might ask her why they're doing a particular thing, and Helen will explain the reason, and then off Hannah will go and do it. When she gets the chance, Helen will ask about it, and when she's too busy she won't. Off the trike, Hannah's ticking things off – she's finished her Master's, and she's quit her note-taking job – but she still needs money, so she's trying to pitch a lot of articles and the like. There'll be a review meeting with Storey Racing to see what's happening next year, and then she's going to go out to Australia for a month, to visit and maybe do some work with a lab at the University of Queensland that looks into muscle function, and do some heat training.

*

... AND BACK TO THE FUTURE

"I just started to get the impression that Hannah wasn't happy," says Helen.

"We see so much of each other, and she's always talking about the coaches she's working with, and what sort of training she's getting, and it seemed like over the last couple of competitions, the relationships just weren't working right for her. I mean, she's had some fantastic coaches, but of course the coach has to fit the rider, doesn't it? So I said look, Han, would you like me to give you some advice? And she jumped on it."

This coach, it seems, fits this rider. "The beauty of having me on board, as I see it, is that I think she feels comfortable telling me exactly how she feels. If you've got a coach that you're not particularly close to, sometimes you don't feel like you can tell them that – so I'd like to think I've calmed her, in a way. She knows I've got her back, and anything I do or say is with good intentions.

"I'm not scared to call her out when she needs that as well, though. Speaking for myself, I know that I need somebody to keep me accountable, and I didn't want Han going off on her own and creating a plan but then not sticking to it because she's got nobody to tell her come on, let's go, let's do this, why haven't you turned up to this.

"Because it's great to have other distractions – like she has had with her Master's, for instance, or her writing. Sometimes, if you've only got one thing, like looking nine months ahead to Tokyo, it can be all-consuming, and it can become a bit daunting. But equally, I think there is a time in a Paralympic cycle where you must prioritise."

They've agreed, for one reason or another, that she's not going to be Hannah's official coach as such – the term they're going for is "performance consultant" – but the main pieces of the relationship are there.

"I'm there for advice. Hannah's all in for this year now – for the past year or so, obviously she's had injuries and operations and stuff, but she's all in for Tokyo, and I really care about her and her performance, so I thought that she deserved to have a plan that was spot on for her.

"So we sat down and worked backwards from Tokyo. I've got the experience on the coaching side, she's got the science, and between us we came up – I think – with quite a good little plan.

"At this point, we have no idea how the selection for the Paralympic Games will go; but what we do know is that the course in Tokyo is going to be extremely difficult. It's going to be very hilly, and the conditions are going to be really tough. So my thoughts were – ok, we need to make you as strong as possible, so you can get up those hills. You need to do more hill climbs, and you need to do some more racing. She's had a period of time without doing a lot of races this season, because of her injuries, and frankly, she needs to race more. So it's about bedding all of that in, so that she can get to next August in the best shape, and able to produce more power than she ever has before. Then the final bit is just mixing the programme up a bit, perhaps a little more than she has been doing – but I think Gary's set Hannah up extremely well for what I've put in place.

"When we sat down together, we were just under a year away from Tokyo. My philosophy in any event is that if you always do what you've always done, you'll always get what you've always got – and looking at the course, and looking at the likely conditions, there had to be changes, because the Paralympic course is like nothing they've ever experienced before, and you can't do what you've normally done anyway – but ultimately, I feel much the same as Gary, really. If Hannah wants it enough, and she commits to the programme, I think she can make the improvements that she needs to.

"What does that mean in terms of result? In all honesty, I don't know. She's there or thereabouts. If she can climb better, she might be able to stay with the main group, and we're working on her sprint, so if she can stay with the top three or four and she can sprint at the end of it, then are we looking at a medal? Maybe."

All of which is quite something to set against Hannah's experience – and, for that matter, her perceptions. Between them, Gary and Helen amount to voices to be listened to. So does Hannah believe them – that a medal is achievable? And if not, is that a problem?

"Honestly," says Helen, "I think when Hannah gets to the racing, she doesn't care. She's a true racer, in that sense. Once she's on the line, you see her face, she's in race mode, and that's fantastic. In a way, because she knows how hard it will be to get near the medals, I think it's making her train even harder. She can't take her foot off the pedals, you know? She's coming from behind. And that's the best place to be in, really. To be the underdog. Because you want it more – you want what others have got."

Does she still have that conviction level? Does she still believe that she could crash, and cross the finish line a split second ahead of Carol because she wants it that bit more? "I really hope so. She wasn't selected for the Para-Athletics Worlds a month or so back, and after all the disappointments she's had this year I did think, oh god, is she just going to say right, that's enough? I've gone through enough, I've tried my best? But I saw a different side to her. She just sat down and said right, I'm going to focus everything on Tokyo – and I thought, fair play. It's there. It's still there."

And why?

"I think she really wants to prove people wrong. She could very easily – and I wouldn't have blamed her at all – have said, I've had enough. I'm going out to Australia, I'm going to do a PhD, and just enjoy my life. But she's committed to it, and that's a big deal. I've been having this chat quite a lot myself recently, me and my team mates, about how intense it is in Paralympic year. To go the last four years waiting for this year to come along is hard. Mentally, it's so hard. And Hannah knows what she's getting herself into, she's done it before, and she's still committed herself. She's said to herself, I'm going to give everything to Tokyo, and then what will be will be. And she'll always know she gave it her all, whatever happens.

"I think it might be just one last shot. And if so, she'll want to prove people wrong. To finish on a high."

The Crash

A bat flaps its wings.

*

PULL YOURSELF TOGETHER

Jess has done it. She's got through 2019, having qualified a boat for the Olympics and knocked off two years of university in one, and she makes the call to defer the next bit of her degree by a year and it's very much the right one.

Because things have gone on a bit of a wobble. Not training – that's started fine – but in terms of normal life, where she's struggling a little bit to get back on the horse.

"I think I just burnt myself out a bit last year," she says. "So it was nice just having a bit of time that wasn't either university or rowing. Reconnecting with friends, not putting pressure on myself, actually recovering from training, that sort of thing."

All of which is fine, but it coincides with a few gentle reminders that it's not quite time to take her eye off the ball just yet. Things like when she goes on a friend's hen do and forgets to change her whereabouts,[1] so when the testers turn up to where she's supposed to be, she's not there, and that's a strike against her and a bit of a ticking-off. Other things, like when around the same time, she picks up both a speeding fine and a parking fine – "Stupid mistakes, because I wasn't really concentrating on where I needed to be. So at that point, it was time just to tell myself ok, pull yourself together, you've still got Tokyo to get through yet."

She's got to get herself there too, of course – there's going to be a British women's quadruple scull competing in Tokyo, but anyone could be in it. So does Jess still think she can go and

---

1. Every day, for an hour at some point between 6am and 11pm, athletes must make themselves available for potential out-of-competition drugs testing – which means recording in advance on a central database exactly where they're going to be during that hour, including hotel rooms, flight numbers, the works. Cock up your admin and miss three tests in a rolling 12-month period, and you're facing a two-year ban from sport.

win gold, like she did when the coaches asked her in Majorca a year or so back?

"Right now, to be honest, I have no idea. A few weeks of good training, and then we'll see where that puts me."

*

EXHAUSTED

Maybe the full PhD that Helen talked about is on hold, but as 2019 comes to a close, Hannah does make it out to Australia for a month.

The IPC has funded several labs around the world to get involved in classification research, and the University of Queensland is one of the main players among them. "I have several possible plans," Hannah says. "It may or may not come off, but one thing that I would love is to become a researcher in cerebral palsy and muscle function. Maybe even an advisor to the Paralympics – to oversee new classifications, or to guide people who want to get stronger, and direct them to the right labs in their area that could help them. I'm not sure exactly what that would involve, but the first step is going to have to be getting a PhD. And normally I have to fight for performance research – the sort of thing I'm interested in – but that's what they're doing here."

So she's come to help out for a bit. And to train, too, of course, because with any luck she's going to be gunning it around a hot and hilly Tokyo in the autumn of 2020, so it'd be foolish to pass up the opportunities offered by a hot and hilly south Brisbane in the southern hemisphere summer of 2019 – but the longer term is very much part of the thought process.

"I'm actually quite scared of the Paralympic blues that I got after Rio," she says. "So my idea is that I get myself a new goal straight away. Like, no time to be depressed, just switch one big project for another. So ultimately, that – well, that and the heat training – was why I was in Australia."

It's been pretty cheap, too.

What she will usually do before travelling somewhere is look up local cycling groups on Facebook – not to ride with them, she'll be too slow, but to find the good routes – and so she's done that, and as luck would have it she's stumbled on a paracycling one. So she's written to them, and within an hour a man called Cam, the only trike rider in Queensland, who happens to stay ten minutes away from the university, has replied, introduced himself by way of a long and jolly essay that's chocka with Australianisms, sent her a picture of a trike with a rainbow on it sitting outside what he's described as "the shack", and invited her to stay with him. Which should, of course, end up saving Hannah a good chunk of money, even if it doesn't quite sound like the safest way of going about things. "There's something about trike riders," Hannah says. "We're a little bit unhinged."

"The shack", as it turns out, amounts to one room. It's connected up to a few others, though, so Hannah gets to know some Zoës and Johns and the like, which is just as well, because Cam's not even there for the first week that Hannah is – he's a little bit more able than her, so he can run, and he's off doing some marathons. Then, when he comes back, he sleeps on a mat on the floor in the corner – it's fine, apparently, with the type of brain injury that he's got, he doesn't really feel pain – and then during the day Zoë and John take Hannah out sightseeing, and Cam shows her all the trike paths he trains on, and off she goes.

"It was the perfect training camp – exactly what I needed," Hannah says. "I cycled everywhere, it was 40 degree heat, and there were loads of good routes, as well as challenging – but climbable – hills. And the lab had a Wattbike.

"Everyone was really open and trusting and friendly, too. I got my Master's result when I was there, and so I gave myself one night to go out on the town. I wouldn't do that back at home, go to a bar by myself, but there, it felt like you could just meet people, get into the community. Just sit at a bar, and everyone talks to you. It was beautiful. Brilliant place."

On the other hand – because maybe there are no uncomplicatedly nice things – there are neck and back spasms to deal with for most of the month that she's there, and massive jetlag when she gets back. "I thought it would cancel out my seasonal affective disorder, but I actually got it way worse," she says. "So when I came home, it was profound, oh god, I've done something horribly wrong. For weeks – and I'm a night owl, I've always been a night owl – I was basically passing out at 7, and falling straight to sleep. So that was a learning experience. And my training definitely suffered."

But she's talking to Helen, and Helen's saying hey, don't worry about it – after all, when you can't do training, it's always for a really good reason, and when you can do training, it's always really good, right? "She made me feel so much better," says Hannah. "She just totally destressed the situation for me. I have to say, with her training, I've not had any of those periods where you look yourself in the face and say, I really can't do this, I don't want to do this. I've had profound periods of fatigue, but I haven't had that."

So the clock ticks round to 2020. With a bit of help from some coffee, she makes it through to midnight on New Year's Eve, which she spends with Elinor Barker and a few of her friends and neighbours, and then suddenly it's The Year, except that she's surrounded by a lot of people for whom, what with being on programme, the Games are a bit more real than they are for her – so the overwhelming emotion isn't so much excitement as sadness.

"I struggle with winter. Apart from being so cold all the time, I'm so distant from any racing or anything that makes me feel like a trike rider, and it feels so lonely. Apart from Scottie, I don't really see anyone else who's a para-cyclist, and it's like, you're not really there. You're not in, you don't see, it's not a thing.

"It just doesn't feel real. For lots of people, they go into their training centre, and they have the whole programme built around them, and it's like, you know where you're going, you know who you're working with... And I really miss that.

"So now what I've started to do – which is not so good, I absolutely get that – is to compare my Rio run-up to the Tokyo one. Because the Rio run-up wasn't good. It was very stressful, but at the end, I was like, ok, I know how it works now. After my last race, as soon as I finished it, I was like, right, I've got four years to do this properly. But instead, it's now a fraction of what the Rio run-up was like, in terms of things like going to a camp every month, having a goal, being involved in something that was as big and meaningful – and just being there, with everyone around me."

But maybe there's one last hope, if she can only get reclassified. Hannah's met up with people from her old gait lab – including her old physio, and the surgeon who's done all of her leg surgery – and it's lovely, because none of them have changed a bit but they've got all this history with Hannah, and they can look at videos of her since she was six, and how far she's come; and long story short, they're not classifiers, but they think she's got spasticity grade three legs.

So maybe she'll get reviewed – if she can convince British Cycling to put her forward – and then at least the classifiers will say whether they think she's still a T2 and why; or maybe they'll say that now she seems to be a T1, but either way, she'll know – and maybe if it doesn't go well she can at least take it up with the UCI, and ask them how many young people have started trike racing and done one race and then had to quit because they've finished miles behind and aren't being classified right.

"I've really tried to work with my classification," she says. "I've really tried. And I really want to believe in the system, but I just don't, any more. So I'm glad I'm making this stand, I guess. Because I never really questioned it. And it's stupid, isn't it, because I know about myself, and my disability, and as soon as they did it, I should have said, 'No, that's not right, I'm a T1. Are you sure?'

"If I'm honest, I can't remember much about the original decision now, but I do remember that I was borderline, and I think they made the decision based on competitiveness, because there was one T1, and they said that I'd do much better in T2 in terms of competition. And to be fair, it made me really strong. But in terms of my actual body, and where it's most fair to go, I think it might be in T1. And if it isn't, and they really have a good argument for that, then great. At least then I've learnt.

"But if anything, if I want to achieve anything in cycling, it might be – no, actually, it is – to make it better for the next generation. I've seen women my age, with spastic diplegia, come into this sport and struggle massively, and maybe they were T1s, or maybe there should be more classifications. Hopefully, by making this stand, it's going to shake things up."

Pending that, though, crack on again with training. Hannah's dad has helpfully just moved to Spain, so that's another broadly affordable unofficial warm weather camp and thank goodness for that, because she's too knackered to be chasing funding right at the moment. Otherwise, training is really about lots of gym work, lots of static bike work. It's basically as high intensity as Helen can get away with in a winter training season, so Hannah doesn't have too much saddle time – partly because, at least for the immediate future, they don't want to destroy her vulva.

Then Spain, big heavy endurance sessions, and then back to strength and high intensity long efforts, with the idea being that they're slowly building things up, making them harder and harder. It seems to be working for the moment – just before Christmas, they were doing some eight minute efforts at threshold, and now they're pushing out the same power at VO2 max – so that's good, and then as winter edges into spring they'll put in big road blocks, lots of miles at low intensity, and then wind that up too once the weather gets better.

How much racing? That depends on whether British Cycling put her forward for review – because in short, she doesn't think she'll be taken to the world championships if they don't. "The benefit of the doubt is the only thing that I think would get me to worlds now," she says. "Because in terms of reclassification, my first opportunity is the next world cup, which is a week before the world championships, and I would need to be assessed twice to get a confirmed classification. So they'll need to select me on spec, essentially. I mean hey, they might select me for worlds anyway? But I do think I need to be sure that I've got more going for me than crashing at last year's worlds on my dodgily positioned trike.

"Do I want to be racing more? Of course. But in terms of my ability to do that, I have so little – few funds, few people. Every year, I've had this ideal plan, and every single year, it just goes tits up. So I'm exhausted. Honestly, I'm exhausted from planning it. So if British Cycling say they want to review me, then great – hopefully they'll take me to the world cup, and then they'll take me to the world championships, and then I'll do Tokyo. And that's about it."

A CHAPTER THAT IS A LOT LESS ABOUT JESS
BEING SELECTED FOR THE OLYMPICS THAN, IN
OTHER CIRCUMSTANCES, IT MIGHT HAVE BEEN

The first knockings of Olympic year, and time for a moment's
reflection. The quad were smashing it in the warm-up camp,
so why didn't that translate? Of course, they qualified the boat,
and of course, that was the main objective, but they were right
up there on percentage gold medal time, so why did other
GB crews come back with medals and the quad trail in sixth?
Maybe it's a peaking thing. Maybe the others built through the
camps a bit slower and then came good at the worlds. Something to look at, perhaps – it could be that they're paddling too
hard, working too hard at lower rates. Hmm.

In the meantime, start the season strong. Avis, twice. For a
while, Jess is being nudged towards a double with Mathilda –
they're being told by the coaches that the decision hasn't been
made about what the top boat is, and so it makes sense to leave
options open in the hope that the double might be able to
pinch a qualifying spot in one of the early season tidy-up races.
It very well could too, because the two of them are going great
guns.

Trials, good, tick. Getting real now. After all this work, all
those injuries, the medals and the losses, the journey – this
journey, at least – is nearly at an end.

Into training on Saturday 21st March. In quite early actually,
and out onto the water with Mathilda, and there's someone on
the bank trying to get their attention, and in they come.

Grab a coat. Here's the team for the Olympics. You're in,
you're out.

Take your ergos, take your weights.

Caversham's closed.

24TH MARCH 2020

Well now, here's a thing.[2]

*

2. www.bbc.co.uk/sport/olympics/52020134

THE LONGEST DAYS

Down the stairs, into the kitchen and over to the cupboard.
  Take out 225 grams of flour.
  Mix with 80g Stork, an egg, and 110 grams of caster sugar.
  Whisk it up.
  Mash four full-on, past their best – no, let's not beat around the bush, *black* bananas, and mix them in, maybe with a bit of orange and lemon zest if you're feeling particularly zazzy. No, there will be no walnuts, fuck you Delia, no-one likes walnuts. No lard, either. Spoon it into a loaf tin, level it off, into the oven at 180 for an hour and ten.
  And repeat.

Tum te tum.

Erm... so... Hannah and her housemate have made it to season 3 of *Buffy the Vampire Slayer*?

He's introducing her to his film collection too.
  Reservoir Dogs is a no.
  True Romance, also a no.
  The original *Ghostbusters* doesn't match up to the remake.
  The Terminator is "clearly just one man's plot to get laid", so she refuses to watch *Terminator 2*.
  Big thumbs up for *Midnight Run*, *Raising Arizona*, *Office Space* and *Spiderman: Into the Spiderverse*.
  Well, what were you up to?

*

IN AN OXFORDSHIRE GARDEN

"When I was a kid, my aspirations were simple. I wanted a dog."
Drive. Longer on the recovery. Drive.

"I wanted a house that had stairs in it – two floors for one family. I wanted, for some reason, a four-door station wagon instead of the two-door Buick that was my father's pride and joy."

Lighter on the arms, come on, come on. Ay ay ay, so many early mornings, so many ergos, this is knackering my back.

"I used to tell people that when I grew up, I was going to be a pediatrician. Why? Because I loved being around little kids and I quickly learned that it was a pleasing answer for adults to hear. 'Oh, a doctor! What a good choice!'"

Fuck me, I've been on this thing for ages, feels like I'm rowing through tar here. Maybe if I face the erg the other way round, have a look at the other end of the garden for a bit, that might freshen things up?

And so the days wear on.

*

LOCKDOWN

Where are you, Jess?
I'm at home, of course.

She's living with Adam these days; and that helps, not least because he's very proactive. Because if on the one hand there's the convenience of being able to get up from the sofa and go straight out to the garden and do your ergo session, on the other there's also the faff of having to actually *get up* off the sofa and go *all the way* out to the garden to do *another* ergo session when you know what, it's not like you're at training like usual with everyone else around to keep you going.

She's a bit worried about weights – about losing her conditioning and power and things like that – especially given that, here at home, she hasn't got many weights to speak of.

But what can you do? You try to stay as fit as you can, and if you can stay pretty fit, then great. After all, it's not like this is something that's buggered up the British, and nobody else. Count your blessings – you can have an ergo at home (and it's not always Michelle Obama in the background, you can switch it up with a bit of a podcast now and then – some James Acaster perhaps, a bit of Matt Lucas), you can have a static bike. Come the evenings, you can keep yourself busy by crocheting a jumper, by knitting a blanket, by taking up calligraphy. It's – well, it's something.

And there's a programme, and a routine. A video call with the scullers every Monday. Then one main ergo session a day, and they kind of mirror what the normal programme would have been in terms of the efforts that you're meant to be putting in. Some people are talking about group sessions, about boat-specific sessions, and Jess has been involved in some of that in her role as an athlete rep, but as far as her own training goes, she just likes cracking on in her own time, working on her own thing, getting it done.

It's a bit of a pisser, because everything else had been set aside in the build-up to 2020, and when you've deferred a year of your degree so as not to have to do it in an Olympic year and then there's a global pandemic and everything and the Olympics gets deferred… But it is what it is.

A month or so passes. Lockdown continues across the country, and bit by bit, everything gets just a little bit harder.

Jess's uncle dies. It's not from Covid-19, but in a way it's even worse, because like her father, it's a heart attack, and it's third generation among the boys. Her great-grandad on her grandma's side, her grandad, and now her dad and her uncle. It's a bit stressful. "I'm not as worried for me," says Jess. "I had palpitations and stuff after my dad died, but looking back, I think it was probably just stress, with training and everything prompting them, because I had every single test under the sun. But I am worried for my brothers – they haven't been tested like I have."

She's also had to work through some difficult feelings about rowing. It's only for about a week or so, but it's like it's been something that she hasn't allowed herself to think about. "I've worked so hard to get to the Olympics," she says. "And it still hasn't happened, and it's now my seventh year, and it's like, how am I even going to know if it's worth it?

"I think, when you're younger, all the stuff you give up isn't that important. You're just like, oh, well, this is fun, and you just kind of do it, and that's that. But then as you get a bit older, things like family and friends and having your own time and space just mean a bit more.

"I'd never forgive myself for just stopping. I knew in my stomach that I would never give up. But to be honest, I went through a period of just fucking hating it."

And British Rowing leave her alone – which in these circumstances, for her, is exactly what she needs. A few different people reach out, and she says thank you, I'll bear it in mind.

She keeps exercising, as far as she can under the rules that everyone has to live with, because that makes her happy. Running with the dog, a bit of paddleboarding along the river at the end of the garden, some cycling. Off-programme, but still going. "It's already mentally tough training in isolation," she says. "So I really didn't want to be forcing myself onto an ergo, or breaking myself into pieces, when I was in that resentful mindset – because then I just knew it would drag on longer." And after a while, she does feel better. Adam's helped. He's kept her laughing, for one – and because he's the practical type, he's also built her a weights rack. "I'm very happy about that," she says. "I can do proper squats, pull-ups, split squats, Bulgarians. I mean, I was doing squats and stuff off bins, but it's so much easier with a rack.

"And I was bending the bins a bit."

There are good things about training like this – not least, a sense of autonomy that wouldn't be there if Jess was training at Caversham. On the other hand, sometimes external motivation is important, whether it's a sense of getting caught up in the programme, or even something as simple as being able to tell yourself, "'Well, if I get this session done, I can go home and have a cup of tea and settle down' – because when you're in isolation you're like, well, I'm already at home, having a cup of tea, settled down…"

That's what it's becoming. Keep on going. Keep on doing what you can while everything changes around you. After the first couple of months, the rules get relaxed a bit, which is kind of good news, but comes with its own oddities and irritants. In May, for instance, rowers are allowed out onto the water, but only if they're "recreational".

"It's a bit frustrating," says Jess. "I've got my boat in my garden, and I'd love to get on the river, but even though most clubs are open – including my club, Leander – at the moment we're not allowed out. I can't go on the river. Because apparently that wouldn't be recreational." Mate, take a sandwich on the boat with you. "I know! Like, guys, I definitely don't do this sport for the money – have you not realised that? I do it because I enjoy it!" So much for marginal gains.

"I do kind of get it, in a way," she adds. "I think one reason why Brendan [Purcell, British Rowing's Director of Performance] has said that he's waiting is because no-one knows the effects of all this socialising until two weeks afterwards. So it's like, let's just hold off a little bit, see what effects it does have, and then we can get going if it's actually safe. So it does make a bit of sense. But I could literally take my single down to the river right now. I'm going out paddleboarding, so what's the difference?

"It's more than that, too. Some of the people at Leander, who are going out on the river, they're still on GB funding. They could get on squad next year. And I brought my boat home – it's kept at Caversham usually, but we're five minutes' walk from the river here, and I brought it home the day that they told us to go, for exactly this sort of situation. So I could just take it."

Basically, this is it. This is the moment, right? This is the moment when, if this was about nothing but winning gold, and pursuing greatness, and being the best you can be, and all

that bullshit – this is the moment when you'd bend the rules.
You'd bend the shit out of them.

"I mean, I absolutely could. I could go out on the river now,
and no-one would really know. But I'm not going to do that.
I want to feel like part of the team. I'm in the team, and if no-
one else in the team can go out, then I won't either."

And you've got to respect that.

*

"MY WHOLE SEASON IS NOW COMPLETELY BLANK"

"How am I doing?" asks Hannah. "Honestly? Not too good."

"There's a plan."
Nope.

In the first few weeks of lockdown, she's crying every half hour. No particular reasons, and just little barks, but it's because she's right on the edge with anxiety, and most of that's coming from a news overload. She doesn't recognise it straight away, but she's reading everything and she's writing some articles too, and her friends can tell that she's getting too involved, so there's a bit of an intervention, and she switches off most of her social media.

"First of all, I show how much I've developed since Harrogate – how I'm not crashing any more, how I'm much faster, back to my normal self. Then I hopefully get reclassified into T1, and then race the T1s, and show how I'm going to get a medal at Tokyo. All of which means doing a really hard eight weeks – because that's when they're going to select for the worlds. I mean, it's synthetic, but do a time trial uphill, a time trial on the flat, a time trial on the static bike, just literally hit all the PBs early, even if it's way out of proportion, just so if they say no, they say no to a real athlete. That would be nice."
Yeah, it would've been.

"Right now, nothing I do is to support anything in the future. My whole season is now completely blank, and it's all about getting through the day – and I've never really been like that before.

"I've always heaped immense pressure on myself. Using my youth and my able-bodiedness while I have it is a really big thing for me. So I used to be very scared of time going by – and now, I'm not. I'm doing stuff to kill time. I never used to be able to do that, and it depresses me.

"I get a big kick out of doing things, out of having goals and working towards something, having a scheme with an outcome. But I'm not doing that. Not at all. I'm just doing the bare minimum. Cook. Plan for cooking. Get into clothes. Have a wash. And I feel trapped.

"I mean, it's complex. Many of my friends have told me that they've completely gone off their trolley. I've had good days and stuff, I'm comfortable, and I've been in much worse situations. But I just don't like stasis, you know what I mean? So physically, I'm comfortable and healthy – but mentally, I'm in anguish."

A few weeks in, and some structure settles on the days – most of them, anyway. There are a few, after Hannah's grandfather dies – and he was 91, and he had dementia, and he'd wanted to go for a long time before he went, but it's still shit, and because of the pandemic they can't even go to his funeral – when she's like, fuck this, I'm spending the day in bed; but she's managed to stumble upon a routine of sorts.

She tells herself she won't do full-on training now that Tokyo's been postponed, and she's seen some evidence that exercising particularly hard could increase the risk of serious complications if she does contract covid – but then she discovers Zwift, and suddenly, she's racing up at her maximum heart rate, pushing out some massive powers, and because there are other people there, she finds herself being taken away from everything else that's going on.

"It was so good," she says, "and so like racing, so like real life trike racing, but without the fear of falling off, so even better in some ways. And there were people of my own ability, because they match you up with people at your power levels. It was really lovely, and suddenly I was like, oh wow, I haven't actually lost my racing for this year!"

So that's what she's doing. There's a bit of outdoor training too, but only once a week, and it's RaceRunning rather than cycling, for a few reasons. It's more efficient, for one – she can only do about half an hour before it starts to hurt – and there's the self-sufficiency element too, given how much experience she's had of punctures, crashes and snapped chains, and how buggered she'd be if she had to deal with them on her own.

But fundamentally it's not about that, not really. It's about Hannah's vulva.

"I'm nervous about the damage I've done already," Hannah says, "and this is a time that I can give it a break – especially if I'm going to be carrying on for another 12 months. In February, when I went to Spain, I did a big bunch of endurance training, but I wasn't wearing my splints. My splints control my hip angle, which decreases the trauma, and without them, it was getting really bad again.

"I've run out of options, really. It was fine when I could tell myself, 'I'm just about to go to the Paralympics, I can just push through until then', that sort of thing, but now I can't, obviously. Twelve months is irreversible. So for now, I've stopped road riding." She's training, basically, towards Zwift races.

Which is good, in a way, because it means that rather than training because she feels that she has to, she's training because it feels good. She's climbed the Alps, she's done group rides, and she's cobbled together a pretty good training pattern, all told. She's doing some gym work in the garden, and she's found herself a virtual support group, "The Para Queens", which essentially amounts to her and a few fellow Paralympians – Karé Adenegan, Ellie Simmonds, Lauren Rowles and Helen Scott among them – training together over a Zoom call.

Sometimes, though, it all feels like therapy's poor relation. Sometimes, says Hannah, "it feels like I'm not doing it for anything, I'm just waiting to get absolutely wrecked, to get too tired to train. Just training out the anxiety."

Twelve more months, then, before Tokyo. But what does that mean? It's not going to be twelve months bursting with opportunities. "It's interesting, isn't it," Hannah says. "Karen Darke is on lockdown in Spain, and she hasn't been able to get out on the road for six weeks. Whereas I could have been, and if we were in the same race, maybe I could have got ahead of her.

"But for me, it's not as simple as that. I don't feel I could go out and do cornering practice, for example, because even though there are beautiful empty car parks, it's not essential, and it feels dangerous. And even if I'm not so much worried for me, Mark, my housemate, is higher risk, and I do worry about him. So a large part of the reason that I do what I do is to keep Mark safe, and to keep people like him safe."

And what of money?

"I've pretty much lost all of my speaking gigs, and a few of my writing opportunities too. Sports grants have dried up – I've lost three of those this season. I've got savings – money that I'd set aside in case of greater disability, basically. Mark and I both have, actually, and we were both like, yeah, this is the time. So I'm getting by through that, and also my spending has gone down – fuel costs is a big one, I drive everywhere, and that costs a bomb. Mark gets free food from the kitchen job he had, so we share food as well.

"I'm still writing two columns, one for *Cycling Weekly*, and another for Paralympics GB; and the podcast that I co-host for the BBC is having a second season, so I'm doing a few episodes of that, and I get paid per episode.

"The writing is getting tricky, but I managed to pull together an article for *Cycling Weekly* about Zwift – because Zwift doesn't have any equality whatsoever. They have zero para-cycling avatars.

"I don't understand why. It's really easy to code, and I've been tweeting them about it for years. They say that making the hand bike, or the trike, is easy – it's coding the aerodynamics that's hard, because they need to get it specific. But as far as I'm concerned, fuck that. It's about representation. If you can't see it, you can't be it. In lockdown, as well, you've got a perfect audience. What if there's a wee girl who has CP, and her dad is on Zwift, but Zwift don't think she can ride a bike, so her parents are like, ok, riding a bike's not for you, let's put you in the swimming pool? When if she could ride a trike, then who knows?"

In the meantime, Hannah's emailed Paula Dunn, head of the Paralympic programme for British Athletics, to ask how things are looking in terms of RaceRunning, and whether and when she reckons it might be put on the Paralympic medal event list, and Paula seems optimistic. As things stand, though, it looks like Tokyo has to go ahead, or be cancelled – closure, one way or another – before they decide the next schedule of events, which is probably fair enough, even if, with good news on that front, it could have been a source of funding. Still, there it is. For the foreseeable future, it's Zwift, it's short bursts of RaceRunning, it's getting through the days.

BACK INTO CAVERSHAM (SORT OF)

Finally, the best part of four months after they were called in and sent away, it's back to Caversham. Of a kind.

It's a trial opening, limited to just seven of them from the Olympic squad for the time being – Jess, Emily Craig, Sam Courty and Annie Withers on the women's side; Tom Barras, Harry Leask and Jonny Walton from the men. Apart from a few of the support staff, that's it.

In they come, one by one, in five minute slots at the gate. Their temperatures are checked, they answer a few questions to flush out any possible symptoms of you-know-what, then into the building; and then for the first few days, it's literally just do your water session, then go home. After a few days, they work it up into a couple of sessions, a bit of work at the UK Sport gyms down the road at Bisham, and then for the last bit it's all of them in together, still socially distancing of course, one-way systems around the building, that sort of thing.

It's been opt-in, and there'll be a chance to opt in or out of coming back when – if? – it opens again fully at the beginning of September. That's pretty much as far as the planning goes, though – there's no provisional calendar for next season, like there normally would be. What could they put in it?

Aside from it being, on the one hand, brilliant to be back actually seeing people in the flesh again and on the other, utterly weird that only a fraction of the usual number are around, the pattern of the few days of Caversham training isn't massively different from what everyone else back home is still up to. Maybe it's a bit easier – the distances they're all doing are about the same, but water miles aren't quite as hard as ergo miles – but that might actually be for the best, as far as Jess is concerned.

"I feel like I've probably lost a bit of strength and fitness.

Mainly due to my personal circumstances, though – if I'd had a smooth ride, I probably would have been in better shape. I've definitely lost some boat skills too. I'm ready to get that back, though, ready to get back on the horse and get that back pretty soon."

There'll be two and a half weeks off, then two weeks of one or two sessions a day, of something to get the limbs moving, whatever they like. Then two weeks of programme-specific training, like what they were doing in lockdown, and then back into Caversham full time, hopefully, for the long push to Tokyo.

*

ISOLATION

Hannah, meanwhile, is still stuck at home.

She and Mark have decided to take things a little bit more like how normal used to be – she's met a friend for coffee, she's been inside a shop.[3] Mark's still high risk, though, so there's only so much she's prepared to do. She's seeing a few people, and she's travelling fairly freely to visit her parents, but each situation requires a bit of a mini risk assessment, and often that will get complicated. "I'm going to see a friend soon, because she's having a garden party for her 30th birthday, but that's still going to be loads of potential vectors. So I'm going to go, because it's her 30th, but it's just a bit like, am I really comfortable with that?"

The saving grace has been the athletics track at Stockport Harriers. Privately owned, fully open air, and until recently one of the few athletics venues that was operational anywhere in the country – which meant that for a little while, it was the place to be for the famous faces – your Hannah Cockrofts, your Sammy Kinghorns.

"I've actually been using it for ages," says Hannah. "For the whole time I've been in Manchester. Because Stockport Harriers are cool, and they were like, yeah, absolutely, here's storage, here's a key, use it whenever you want. Brilliant. Before all of this, I would generally try to go when other people are there – health and safety, that sort of thing. But then cue lockdown, and suddenly I couldn't go there at all. So I took my RaceRunner home.

"Then all the cars disappeared, and for a while it was beau-

---

3. Which is, of course, slightly less of a change from how things used to be for Hannah. As she points out, if you don't have reliable legs, you don't just pop down the road for a pint of milk.

tiful. Run round the neighbourhood. Perfect, safe, fine. But as soon as the government decided that open air environments were ok, then the traffic also came back, so it was no longer safe to run the roads. So I sent an email to Stockport Harriers saying, hey, yeah, I'm going to get run over... can I come and use the track? And they said yes. They wrote up a risk assessment, someone did a rota, and there's all the paint and all that to say which way round you go. It's great."

Good thing that it's there too, because there don't seem to be many other opportunities around. "British Cycling have nothing to do with me any more," Hannah says. "They've totally wiped me off the surface of the earth. And the UCI, who govern Paralympic cycling – they haven't been organising anything either. So bottom line, there's no hope of racing."

She's spoken to John Lenton, para-cycling pathway manager at British Cycling, but what she's hearing from that side seems pretty clear, and that is: stop. There's no hope. You're never going to get back on. Hannah might have a better chance if she wasn't a T2 – but to have any chance of becoming a T1, she'd have to be racing.

There's a bit more back and forth on the call with John – could I be doing anything other than I am at the moment? Not really. How's your twenty minute power output looking? Yeah, pretty stable actually. At the end of it all, though, it's pretty clear that that's it. Twelve months or so, give or take, from lockdown to maybe there's a vaccine, and over that time, as far as Hannah's concerned, "I have less than no support."

Maybe it's good, in some way – at least to have thrashed that out, because it's given her some closure. "I wanted to be released," she says. "I wanted to be released from having to work to try and get back on a programme that just doesn't value me in any way. And luckily, that's how it felt. By the end of the conversation, it was clear that it was going to be pointless – I mean, obviously they can't say that outright, but it felt very clear to me by the end.

"The brilliant thing about elite sport, the thing I love, is working with professionals, all together, in order to develop parts of myself that I can't do alone – because it's too much. I can't do it all alone. So I had one last shot, one last chat. But now that's it."

So where does that leave things?

Mike and Charles are still around, and they're working on a new trike – which Hannah was supposed to be training on, but is somewhere in Newcastle right now, in pieces, and what with the pandemic and all that, Mike's a bit stuck for the moment.

Maybe the gym, then. That is, not the *actual* gym, the *gym* gym – that's not happening either – but some bands in the garden. No equipment from British Cycling, obviously, so if there's something you're after, you're on the same exercise gear websites as literally everyone else because you know what, we're all stuck at home now, and no-one's getting the exercise that they used to. All of which isn't even to take into account that Hannah needs a bit of help in manoeuvring gym stuff, so all in all she hasn't really been able to do any real weights.

A coach? Not really. Obviously, there's been Scottie, but this is more about someone who could actually be there, in person, in case of emergency, and the pandemic is making that a bit tricky, too. And other things are falling back a bit, like her position – "I've not been comfortable at all," she says. "Loads of people have tried to sort my position, but I'm at a point where I need the help of a physio and an engineer who would work together with a bike positioner to make sure that I'm in a position that's both aerodynamic and also won't tip me off the bike. That's the thing, and I can't crack that myself."

So she's doing what she can, which is mostly Zwift, keeping the power up. "Everything else is going by the wayside – but I don't beat myself up about it. It's how things are for now."

Maybe there could be something in terms of diet, because Hannah's reached a point where her twenty minute powers, whatever gets thrown at them, seem to be plateauing. "I'm starting to think that's because of my disability," she says. "I can't go any higher. I can't make my muscles any more developed than they are. But what I can do is, I can lose a bit of weight. So I've been working with a nutritionist. I've got these twelve months or so now, and Tokyo's going to be super hilly, so I thought, if I can keep it healthy, then maybe that would increase my climbing ability. Keep the powers the same, but then increase the power-to-weight ratio.

"So the idea is that I work on that, and then get this trike, and get the jump on that... but you know what the thing is? You know what the real, stupid thing is? It's money. Again. Because it's twelve months, and I've had to part ways with Storey Racing, so I'm not going to get any funding from them."

The problems on that front started before the pandemic, when Sarah said that she couldn't fund Hannah to race the world cup in Italy, and that for that matter she wouldn't actually be able to fund any future para-cyclists going to world cups, because of something to do with how the UCI wouldn't put the Storey Racing name on any of their communiqués. Which might of itself have been fine, but then Sarah also wanted the team to do a bit of a social media push, promoting the opportunities for Zwift racing, keeping it positive, keeping people's spirits up, and that didn't sit well with Hannah. "She was saying things like, 'Don't post anything political. Only post positive stuff.'

Which made me think, hey, do you know me, Sarah? I mean, positive is fine, but I'm not doing anything performative. If I feel bad, and I want to tell people, I think it would be a disservice not to say that, to say actually, everyone, this is how things are. It made me think that we were at cross purposes a bit; and one thing led to another, and bottom line, we're not working together any more."

So she bombards a whole load of potential sponsors, and nobody is interested. It's tricky at the moment, of course it is, with no imminent prospect of racing to give a return on investment, but could one of them maybe say that they'd be up for covering race costs in twelve months' time? No, apparently not. Hannah tries to shrug it off – "my thing isn't being the face of a brand, anyway. I'm too individual for that. Or stubborn, maybe" – but it does rankle, and it's another layer of anxiety.

"I don't know where my life's going to go now," she says. "I don't have a clue. I'm just training, but even that's super isolating, so I know that I can't just train any more. I haven't even been on the Para Queens WhatsApp group recently. I mean, at the start, it was cool, it was motivational, we'd do our sessions and sometimes Lauren Rowles, the rower who started it, she would give some good tips. But as it's gone on, it's got harder and harder.

"And it's everything else, too. I've struggled to write. I've distanced myself more and more from social media. I've stopped Zoom calling people.

"I drove to Birmingham, to see Scottie in her garden, but otherwise no-one's around. All of my normal support network in Manchester have moved back to live with their parents, so it's been a real struggle. I'm an extrovert, other people are where I get my joy. Before all of this, I'd be seeing at least one person a day, if not two. I don't like the inside of my head."

But that's where she's stuck, for now. She's been coaching

herself, setting her own training programme on Training-Peaks, and the only regular contact that she has with a professional is her nutritionist, a man called Charlie Mitten. He makes sure that she fuels every session properly, and when she's doing her sessions, that helps her feel very prepared.

"At the moment, that – that structure – that's what's holding me together."

*

FORTNIGHT BY FORTNIGHT, DAY TO DAY

A short holiday, tooling around with Adam, and then back into training again.

The first couple of weeks are away from Caversham, from wherever suits people best: as long as everyone is somewhere in the UK, it doesn't matter. As Jess understands it, that's because they would normally have had a couple of months off around now post-Tokyo, but of course Tokyo hasn't happened yet. So it's a way of giving them some extra time, like they would have done, but still getting back into it. Jess goes up to see her mum, and she and Holly Nixon have a bit of a northern training camp, some ergo work, some cycling.

It goes down well with Jess, even if it's less about time off than about having the mental freedom to do her training wherever she wants; and then it's a couple more weeks of everyone training out of their own homes, a British Rowing–imposed self-isolation period to make sure that nobody brings covid into the training centre.

When they do come back, as a full squad this time, it's on a rota. Each day, there's one session at home – an ergo session, or some cross-training – and weights and a water session at Caversham, with an early shift and a late one, one week at a time on each, which means that there's only ever about twenty rowers on site. Within the scullers, there might be a bit more time in singles than there used to be, but they're still trying to do a bit of all of it, while sticking as far as possible to the precautions of the outside world – socially distancing as much as possible, wearing face coverings. Wiping down the weights bars between every set, and cleaning everything after they've finished; so if someone has to go off – and touch wood, it's been a couple of months and there hasn't been anything within the team as yet – the rest of them can keep on coming in as long as they haven't actually been in a crew boat together.

In a strange way, the fact that the UK goes into another national lockdown on Hallowe'en makes life a bit easier, because they're allowed to carry on training – they need to wear their kit on the way in, and they've got letters from British Rowing in case they get stopped – and at least in theory, it should make them a bit less likely to catch the virus from someone else.

So on they go. It's fortnight by fortnight planning at the moment, with a target piece or two to keep the juices flowing – a cross-squad 5k ergo test, that sort of thing – but there's no calendar for the season like there normally would be, and no published strategy for Olympic selection, because nobody really knows what the early part of next year is going to look like. There is some racing among the squad, but it's not going to be used in selection, and there's a camp in Avis pencilled in for early January, but it's going to be voluntary – not least because they'll be flying commercial rather than chartering a plane – so the coaches have had to be clear that opting out isn't going to harm anyone's chances of going to Tokyo. Which seems fair enough, given that they've recently opted the whole squad out of going to Poznań for the European Championships.

"There was actually never any talk among the squad about doing the Europeans," says Jess. "We heard that it was happening, but the management just decided straight away to not go, with covid still being a massive risk. And then we heard about quite a few athletes getting it while they were there, and athletes knowing that they were unwell but still wanting to race and being allowed to race. So for me, it was definitely the right decision not to do it.

"Even if we had been given the option, too, the quad group's changed so much again. Melissa's gone over to sweep – I think she's always felt a bit more comfortable in a sweep boat, that's how she got into the team – and Mathilda wasn't in the first couple of weeks, and then Holly's had to manage her health situation, doing whatever it is she needs to do to start her season the best. So it did feel like, we just need to focus on ourselves, really. Just building our crew, working on team dynamic and things."

Same as it ever was. This is not Poland, this is not the Netherlands, this is another season, and another new combination in the British boat. It's not going to contain Beth – her back problems turned out to be related to endometriosis, and she's now retired from rowing and is teaching swimming; it's not going to have Zoë – she's just retired too; and it's not going to have Melissa; but maybe it'll be carrying Kyra Edwards, or Saskia Budgett, or Charlotte or Holly or Mathilda or who knows who else. At the moment, it feels like it could be any of them. Who would Jess put in the boat if she had to select it now? "Honestly, I have no idea. I don't even know if I'd put myself in it!"

Well, at least the other countries won't know what to expect.

And for now, Jess seems to be coping with the uncertainty of everything – as well as anyone, that is. "It's hard sometimes," she says. "Because there's still that doubt whether the Olympics are even going to be on. But then I think I'd want to carry on rowing anyway, even they didn't happen. So yeah, generally, I'm fine. Right now, it feels like I've had my wobble.

"I mean, you've just got to see what happens, don't you? At the moment, I may as well just train like it's happening – and things do seem to be getting a bit better all the time. The coaches are keeping the programme interesting, it's not just the same two weeks on repeat. The Avis camp is something to aim towards, but I don't feel like I'm in need of it, as such.

"If you told me now that Tokyo was cancelled, and I was training towards Paris, would I be in a different head space? Yeah, probably. But for the moment, I'm just looking more day-to-day. I think that's all you can do, really."

*

WHEN I WAS HAPPIEST

A job! And not just any job, either, but a Very Important one, as a Covid-19 contact tracer.

"I don't really know anything about it," Hannah admits, shortly after successfully applying for it, "beyond that it's essentially calling people, and that some spreadsheet expertise might be needed. But most of the rest of my income has dried up, and I obviously don't have Storey Racing to fund next season. I don't even know what next season will be, if it will be RaceRunning or cycling or nothing at all – so in short, I definitely need to work this winter."

It's the culmination of a long process – given everything that's been going on, or perhaps more pertinently, everything that hasn't, she's been trying to get employed for a good six months. There have been a few different possibilities, but nothing has come through until now, when she's seen the advert and thought, yeah, I could do that. I could tell people they've got the coronavirus. And compared with the rest of her employment history, it's got one huge perk.

"It's stable," she says. "I'm contracted on a full time basis, and for a year, or as long as it remains relevant. I've never had a non-zero hours contract job before, a job that's actually stable like that. Certainly compared to freelance journalism – which, frankly, sucks ass. So while I can't honestly say that I'm excited about it, I'm also not unhappy. We'll see how it goes."

There's still some time spare for training, and she's made the decision to switch the emphasis from endurance to sprint – which in practice means a fair bit of RaceRunning, a Thursday cycling time trial and a three to four hour ride on a Sunday. There are a few reasons behind the change – for one, it's a lot less fatiguing, but also, maybe there's a permanent switch back to RaceRunning coming sooner rather than later.

They've already got top-level races going again, even if Hannah hasn't gone to any yet – "I'm not going to infect everyone just to get some times on" – and Paula Dunn is in regular contact, checking how she is; and after a while of this, Hannah has a thought and says, actually, Paula, I don't have a coach at the moment. Would you be able to look over my programme? And sure enough Paula says that she will, and that she won't make Hannah give up cycling to do it, so she's coming to the track to help out; and what's more, she now seems to be very confident that RaceRunning will get confirmed for Paris 2024, maybe as early as next January. Which puts Hannah in a great position in terms of funding, provided that her times are in the top five or so in the world – which they almost certainly will be.

So let's see. "I do want to be there at the trike qualification event for Tokyo, as and when that comes around," she says. "But it depends. It depends where I'm living. It depends what support I get. It depends if this supertrike that Mike's building is ready, and it depends on whether I can do anything more with my powers. I'm maintaining my twenty minute power level, and maybe I can go beyond that, but I'm not going to be able to do that unless I have an event to target. Something to try to peak for." And what's that event going to be? She doesn't know, not yet – it might be the world championships in early June, but that won't be confirmed until about a month before.

There's a lot to think about more broadly too. "I'm a T2," she says. "My re-classification isn't going to happen, so realistically, I have to just see what shape I'm in next year, in terms of whether I can keep this going. I really want to do Tokyo. I've not given up that dream. At the same time, though, there are certain ways I want to live the large part of my life – which isn't just the month of the Paralympics – and that is not chasing after a governing body or even doing a lot of fruitless cycling training that just exhausts me. In fact, the more I think about it, I actually think that maybe the way I'm going to improve my performance is by doing the mix of sports, and always was. That's when I was happiest, certainly. I don't know."

So on with the sprint training; and if she's honest with herself, is all of this about RaceRunning, in the end? "I want to get my 100m world record back," she admits. "For sure. But who knows? What if it doesn't get a medal event in January, or if the decision is postponed? Whether I really want to get the world record back in 2021 specifically, I'm not sure. Right now, I'm just doing something to pay the bills, and I won't be able to do much endurance training alongside this work week. It's just how it's going to have to be, with no funding.

"And I know the winter is meant to be about endurance, but even in that one season, with John Hampshire, where I'd done a lot of endurance training, was the fittest I ever was, and had a really good set of races, they still weren't the best. Frankly, there've been lots of ways I've tried it, and none of them have worked.

"Year after year, I've trained towards keeping a high enough aerobic threshold to be there at the sprint – which is fine, but then obviously I'm never there at the sprint, even when I've been at my fittest. So basically, I'm going to need to revisit everything again, once I've got a clearer picture of things – and that's probably going to be in January."

In the meantime, what that all means in practice is a lot less time spent training – and not only that, but some saved around the edges too. "Endurance training means a lot of planning," says Hannah. "A lot of planning, and a lot of preparing food and eating. A lot of mental fatigue, too, because you have to break through those barriers along the way. So with me needing to do a job as well as train, sprint is the best way."

There has, at least, been one very positive development – another new saddle from Specialized. "It's ridiculous, honestly, it's the most ridiculous thing," says Hannah. "It came from Alan Murchison, who is this very cool guy who went from Michelin starred chef into sports catering. He does loads of social media for Specialized, and he was testing out this 'mirror' saddle, and he said it was too soft, didn't work. I was like, 'Alan, too soft? That's perfect! Can you send it to me, can I try it?' Because the market price is huge.

"And he just sent it to me. I tried it, and I loved it so much. It was so comfortable. So I got in touch with my contact at Specialized, and I said, 'Look, I know it's massively expensive, but can I try it? I'll write you something until the price is paid off, whatever.' And she just sent me one of their marketing ones, that was a bit bashed up, and was like, don't worry, we just want you to be comfortable. You don't have to do anything at all. Which I guess is one of the advantages of having no social media following!"

So she's come around to feeling, overall, pretty good. Working with Paula is going well, it feels like they're tracking changes ("that's what I live for, working towards something"), and it may be chipping away at her endurance, but she's been going fast in her recent road rides.

Of course, there could be all sorts of reasons for that. Maybe she's just finally got over her injury, maybe it's this new saddle, or maybe it's her trike set-up – she's back to how she started in terms of position, but for the time being at least, she's not causing herself the same health issues that got her into the national newspapers.

Targets? Who knows; but she doesn't feel like she's going for gold any more. "I don't know what else I can do," she says. "It's going to be maybe a bronze, if things go my way. I don't think I can really get much else out of my body, unfortunately, that I haven't already. I think that once you've done it year after year, it's pretty easy to ping back to where you were – so I can get back to where I was, and maybe a tiny bit higher – but even if I gave up everything else and just did cycling, I think gold's probably out of reach.

"Looking back now to the start of the winter of 2019, I specifically quit my job, and apart from a couple of writing and podcast things, pretty much dropped everything else – to make sure that when it came to this summer, I didn't have anything to juggle. And then, of course, everything changed.

"It does feel, though, a bit like I'm re-energised, and ready to go again. I'm going to have this winter as a juggling winter, and then we'll just have to see. I might turn up to a race and be absolutely epic because I've had this long period with no racing, no aiming for the crazy powers that I used to aim for; and while Jon Pett has always said that they don't just want to fill the places at Tokyo and that they only want to take gold medal winners, sometimes they don't have gold medal winners to fill the places, so maybe there'll be space for me.

"Because the thing is, I am an elite athlete. I've kept my performances up, and we'll just have to see what I'm capable of logistically. It's not really 'why I do sport' – I do sport to be bloodthirsty and win all the things – but competition's been taken away from me entirely, and so it's kind of out of my hands.

"So I'm not going to stress about it, because it's really hard, and I don't have any support. I'm just going to focus on the RaceRunning, enjoying the cycling, keeping my skills up, keeping my steady state power, and let's see what happens when I get shot out the other end."

The End

She laughs — sort of.
And she says no.
Let's not do that.

*

"WHAT'S THE POINT ANY MORE?"

Winter comes, and it's not dicking around. Across the country, it's cold and it's shit, and you can kind of see why the government wanted, for a while, to allow people to meet up with their families over Christmas, because this has all been going on for quite some time now, and it's shit, and it's cold.

But the case numbers spiral upwards again and that's not what happens, and so Jess and Adam – who'd actually decided already that they weren't going to travel up north and visit her mother, because they'd thought it would be safer not to – stay at home and catch covid.

She'd just recovered from a rib injury, so had taken her boat home with the thought that she could put in a big block of training and start to catch herself up a bit. Then, about two days after Christmas, she started feeling tired, it got worse the day after that, and sure enough the covid test came back positive.

"The first few days were all right – it just felt like a mild flu," she says. "But then things went pretty rapidly downhill. I couldn't do anything – even something like washing the dishes would make me sweat. I struggled with my focus, I couldn't concentrate, pretty much all I could do was just sit in front of the TV. And then I completely lost my sense of taste and smell, and that really got to me. Literally, could not smell or taste anything. Couldn't have a cup of tea to cheer myself up, nothing. I couldn't be bothered to eat – I would just eat to stop my stomach hurting, and that was that. It was horrendous."

Adam gets it too – but while they're feeling about as bad as each other, she's dealing with it worse. "I was so irrational," says Jess. "Properly like, 'I'm never going to be able to enjoy a family meal again! I can't just sit there watching everyone else enjoy their food. What's the point any more?' Because normally, when you're ill, you can have a cup of tea, something that you enjoy, to make yourself feel a bit better – but when you lose all of that, it just feels like nothing gives you joy."

A week or so of this and Jess is telling her better judgment to stick it, and is scrolling desperately through Google to see if there's anything that she can do to bring her smell and taste back, or if there's anything that she is doing which might be making things worse. Which means, of course, reading all the stories about how there are some people who never get them back, but that's only a bit stressful, it's the internet, and then Ann Redgrave, the team doctor, asks how she's doing, and Jess says, yeah, I'm doing all right, but this smell and taste thing is really getting me down, and Dr Ann says yeah, and you know what, there are some people who never get them back.

Which is not what she wants to hear from a highly respected medical professional.

After a few weeks, the taste and smell start to return; otherwise, though, progress is unpredictable. A bit better, and then crash, a bit better, crash. Eventually, Jess builds back into training, gets up to two sessions a day, except that she finds that she can't then cope with normal life. "I'd get home and wouldn't be able to keep my eyes open. I'd just have to crash out for hours and sleep." She's more than happy to make that sacrifice, but the coaches and the medical staff aren't, so she gets cut off completely from exercise for a week, which is a bit crap, and it's another step or two backwards.

Even learning that lesson isn't quite enough, and soon, something else has to give. "I've had to defer my degree another year," she says. "In the early stages, I obviously couldn't row or do any exercise, but on top of that, I couldn't do any university work – and usually, that's what helps me through times with injury and illness. I can get quite a bit done.

"But both were just building up. For the first few weeks, whenever I put more energy into studying, even if I just exerted myself a tiny bit too much, I then couldn't row. And that's my job. That's what I get paid for. So I need to make sure I get that one right."

Which means taking her covid properly seriously, shutting out the noise and listening to exactly what it's saying to her. Because it isn't, and hasn't been, fair – it's hit others in the squad, and they're all fit and healthy young athletes, and some of them have brushed it off and been fine, and some just haven't. Over on the sweep side, there's one who got it pretty early on and is still suffering, month after month fighting fatigue, unable to return to training – which serves to emphasise to Jess how fortunate she's been. This doesn't just top out at something like a bad flu. It can mean lung scarring. It can mean worse.

"I do feel really lucky," she says. "Even though in terms of rowing I'm not where I want to be, I've still got my health, I can still exercise. I'm still here.

"And bit by bit, my energy has come back. For weeks, even though I was going into training and getting through the sessions, I literally only had energy for that. And I know this sounds really dramatic, but it isn't – I remember having the energy to feel happy again. I remember dancing in the car on the way to training one day, and I always do that, normally, but I just hadn't for ages. I hadn't had enough energy to be able to goof around. So it feels like I'm finally getting back to more like my normal self."

Back into full training, even if getting up to racing fitness is going to take a bit longer – which is to say that coming into springtime she's not symptomatic for acute covid, and hasn't been for a while, but she's still working on getting her body recovered enough to train on top of that. "It's been like nothing I've ever had before," she says, "but at least this final bit feels a bit like a normal recovery from injury or illness. Building up the effort, keeping an eye on my heart rate, that kind of thing."

She's also been doing a lot on the mental side – things like writing down how she wants to feel when she's back in the boat, and what technical elements she particularly wants to hold on to; and she's been speaking to the team's psychologist about visualisation.

"Some of it's really hard to explain without sounding weird," she says. "Like, in the recovery visualisation, you imagine a light moving through your body, and then getting to a part that you need to heal, or that you want to feel better in, and things like that. Or there's a rowing-specific one – you start with picturing your boat, and you walk over to it, that whole process, and then you visualise your rowing after that, and how it feels. What you see, what you hear. What the technical things would look like, and how they would feel. The idea being that your mind's then already been through it, so it comes more naturally when you get back on the water.

"It goes wider than that, too – about being grateful for your body, and the fact that it can take you all around the world, and produce power that most people will never achieve. Not blaming your body, just being patient with it. A bit of mindfulness. I've been doing a lot of mindfulness apart from that actually, outside of the programme, and it's really helped me."

Of course, for all that she's been doing what she can, it's still now March in an Olympic year and it's still been two months and more out of the boat; but at least the chance has finally arrived for Jess to catch up on some water time and to embed some technique changes – notwithstanding that it was those same changes which had knacked her rib before Christmas.

They've been in the name of stroke efficiency – bringing more of the effort down from the traps[1] to the lats[2] – but change has come at a cost. "A rib stress in our sport is a repetitive, overuse thing," says Jess. "So if a change in technique means that I'm loading slightly differently off every catch, but I'm not quite strong enough, or something just gives way quite easily around there, then that's what's going to happen.

"I'm obviously a bit weak around those areas anyway. I've had a lot more rib stresses in my career than most people. In fact, other than colds, rib injuries are probably what has taken me out of rowing more than anything else. But at least after this one I look different in my technique, which the coaches think is a positive."

Before the covid, she was managing herself pretty well – training on the bike, keeping fit, with an eye on going out to Avis in January and training completely normally through that, with lots of racing to look forward to at the end. But as it happens, she's not the only one who's had problems. Covid, low vitamin D, a jaw operation here and a back injury there, and there are only four scullers who manage to make it out on camp at all – Holly, Charlotte, a new squad member called Hannah, and Vicky Thornley.

That's where this quad's been for the past four and a half years, though, and that's where it is now. With any luck, five or six of them will be fit for the European Championships in

---

1. Trapezius muscles – the top bit of your back, basically. The bit you use to shrug.
2. Latissimus dorsi. A bit lower down, and off to each side. Does lots of work with your arms.

April – and you'd expect that the coaches will be desperate to give race experience to anyone who can make it, given how long it's been since they had any international competition at all – but Jess needs to have completed four weeks of the normal programme before she'll be allowed to race, so it's almost certain that she won't be going. "I'm only on a slightly modified programme at the moment," she says, "so it depends. But either way, I should still be able to do some kind of performance piece. Like, there are a few people doing a 2k on that weekend, a 2k ergo, that are staying at home. Or if I get back a bit quicker, I could maybe be taken as a spare, but I suspect that that would be because they literally didn't have anyone else.

"To be honest, right now I don't feel like it'd be in my best interests to race so quickly anyway, and also, it wouldn't be fair on the girls that have actually done the seat racing this time, and trials that I haven't done. So yeah, I think I'm coming to terms with it. I'm happy with the trajectory that I'm on, I'm hitting the numbers they want me to, I've been doing some short bursts in crew boats, and I do feel so much stronger week on week. So I'm looking forward to being ready when I'm ready, and putting up a performance when I need to."

And there will come a time in the not too distant future when she will very much need to, because there's going to be more testing within the team after the Europeans, pretty much entirely for the benefit of the quad. "All the other crews are kind of sorted, I think, and the last bit of testing should already have been completed, really," says Jess. "But we're a bit of a mess. At least this season we're only doing the Europeans and one world cup, though, so there's still time to sort it all out."

For the sake of her rehab, the medical staff have told her not to worry. Take your time, they've said. You've got until just before the Olympics if you need it, they've said. Let's be honest, though. The coaches – especially with this quad's history –

aren't going to want things to still be up in the air two or three weeks before Tokyo. They're going to want to find some way of getting the same four scullers to sit in a boat together for a couple of months.

*

LIVING ARRANGEMENTS AND LIVER FAILURE

"I'm not unhealthy," says Hannah.

"I feel fine," she says, despite the blood tests which are apparently showing signs of liver failure. Sometimes sportspeople have liver function test results that are slightly off, she explains, albeit usually that's one or two markers, not, you know, all of them.

She doesn't think she's accidentally given herself hepatitis. Maybe it's just a sign of unhappy muscle, she says – "spasticity plus crazy amounts of exercise followed by sitting cramped at a desk." It might just be her natural physiology, or it might not even be about liver function at all – it might be a sign of something else.

Hmm.

Meantime, she's moved back to Glasgow. There are a few reasons why, one of the main ones being that, through Scottish Cycling and the Scottish Institute, she can get access to a gym – so finally, after more than half a year away and with less than twelve months until the Paralympics, gym is now twice a week again, one-on-one with a man called Ryan who's kitted up in all sorts of PPE. And how is it exactly that she's got access, when she couldn't be further away from the minds of the big cheeses? "Because" – at least, this is the story that she can tell through Scottish Cycling – "I'm going to Tokyo. Because I'm *going* to Tokyo," she says. "The world cup bronze medal I got back in 2019 goes a long way."

Glasgow life is not quite what it might be. She can't find an accessible house with affordable rent, so she's back with her parents – and her parents are lovely, but she's still 27 – and with the Scottish winter comes the sheet ice, so she's barely able to walk outside her front door, and every time it snows, there's one day of the good crunchy stuff and she can stay upright and the rest of the time is, well, not that, and then there's massive flooding, not to mention the cycle paths that are fine as far as they go except that they're not wide enough for a trike, and the snow sweepers can't clear them, and there are massive bollards everywhere – but she finds a way, and between powering through 80km, 100km sessions on Zwift and finding some good roads where she can keep her eye in, she's kept going.

Of course, with Gavin and Kayleigh and the club and everything, Glasgow should be the place to be for RaceRunning too, but it's more difficult than it perhaps needs to be to get track access. Things are obviously a lot harder without Janice and Ian, who's moved away to grieve, and while there are a couple of people in particular, John Owens and Caroline Johnston, who've been doing the best they can, it's been an uphill struggle, because everyone's still waiting for a decision about RaceRunning and Paris 2024, and because everything's taking a hit financially because of covid. "So it's just a complete mess," says Hannah. "And to be organised and get on top of my training, as well as having a full time job? It just didn't work. So slowly, we – Gavin, Kayleigh and I – just had less and less access. Since the worst of the snow and ice has hit, I've basically not been RaceRunning at all."

And so sure enough, Paula Dunn has encouraged Hannah to concentrate on cycling in the lead up to Tokyo, which feels a shame. "I wanted to keep my foot in with RaceRunning, because I wanted to be part of that team," says Hannah. "But it does feel like I'm being let down by the process, and how it treats sports that don't have a medal event. To be honest, I cannot believe that just because I do cycling, and cycling is a Paralympic sport, I get the kind of access to training support that

Kayleigh Haggo, who's a world champion, doesn't. I can't get over that injustice."

So with RaceRunning having to take a back seat, what has she been doing? Well, forty hours a week of work, for a start. "The job gives me a sense of purpose," she says. "I'm doing something and I'm getting feedback on my performance, which is pretty cool – and at least I now know that I have proper transferable skills.

"When you've been doing sport, and you've been in that bubble for so long, then if you're not getting brand deals and things like that, you're kind of sacrificing your whole young working life. It's quite scary to look that in the face and think, ok, I'm choosing to do elite sport, but what that means is that I will have to start from ground zero afterwards. Whereas this way, at least I'll have done six months of work."

The money helps too, of course. "Not getting money for what I'm putting time into has been a constant source of worry. Ever since I started this cycle, the need to fund my season – it's been so draining. People know that, that's why there are disability sports funds, but doing it for this long..."

And she is enjoying the job. It has its downsides, spending so much time sitting down and hunched over – "I'm really worried about what it'll do to me physically, to have a desk job. I've been in so much pain" – but on the other hand, it's been quite challenging, so she's not got bored. But it's not where she wants to go with her life.

Looking towards Tokyo, then. For all that Scottish Cycling are putting the brave face on, this might yet all be for nothing, but as she says, "I committed to this, and I'm still committed to it. I know what I need to do to get to the world cup in Belgium, and then we'll see how I do, and we'll go from there.

"I mean, I'm still worried. For instance – and especially without British Cycling support – I'm worried that I might just get stopped, and be unable to compete, because we can't get into the country or something. So as positive as I sound, I've been wracked with anxiety – and probably will be again tonight, now that I've been talking about it! But it's the life now."

For the next few months at least, it's cycling all the way. She hasn't done any power tests for a while, but she should be there or thereabouts given the work she's been putting in. She's stopped working with her nutritionist, because with the recent liver issues, she's worried that she might be putting too much pressure on herself ("My plan was to lose weight up until the Paralympics, so I could get up the hills faster," she says, "but then because of this health thing, we just put the weight straight back on – and there's no point working with a nutritionist if you don't have a goal"), and she's just trying to do some training pretty much every day, usually before work – a gym session here, a double day there, the occasional rest day, but otherwise an hour or more of exercise, adding up to about ten hours per week – which feels like a lot on top of a full time job.

A block of heavy over-training, to squeeze the last bits of fitness, and then some over/under sessions – the threshold work she was doing with Gary – as well as some sprints and cornering as the roads begin to dry out and things build up towards Belgium. She's keeping a detailed log of everything she's been up to, with the thought that that might help Scottish Cycling to make a case to British Cycling to say, 'Take her to Tokyo, this is what she's been doing', but she's not had time to seek out any meaningful feedback on it all. "They might say, 'That's absolute shit!'" They might indeed, Hannah. We'll just have to see.

And what of Tokyo itself? For Hannah, if on the one hand there might be a question mark over the ethics of putting on a major international competition in the middle of a pandemic, on the other there's no doubt as to what she'll do if she gets the chance. "If I get there, if they give me the ticket, I'm going to take it. I'm not going to say, oh no, I'm morally against this. I'll go, I'll spend ten days in the hotel beforehand to quarantine or whatever, because that's what the point of all of this is.

"Covid's going to be ongoing for a while, but I'm much more confident about how to manoeuvre within that now, and in the processes that are being set up to mitigate risk. Bottom line, I'm happy to just go full throttle."

If it does happen, it's not going to be the full-on Paralympic experience. But then, it probably wasn't going to be anyway, for one reason or another, and actually, it kind of wasn't last time either. "The one thing I would be sad about is not getting to meet other people from different countries," she says, "but because they were already going to be putting us in a satellite village, that probably wasn't going to be a possibility in any event. We'll be shuttled to the race, the only connection that we'd have to other people is while we're actually racing, and even the podium will be socially distanced, so I wouldn't be able to enjoy that in the same way either. And realistically, I'm not going to be able to have my parents there. It'll be totally plastic. But I still would want to do that."

Not least because in many ways, that's pretty much how it felt five years ago. "I felt so disconnected from everything and everyone back then. Even if there are fewer, or even no fans there this time, that wasn't very different in Rio. I could hear my parents echoing on the tarmac, shouting, 'Go Hannah!' And then a pause as they ran round... 'Go Hannah!'

"So I need to do the Paralympics, if I can. It might turn out that I can't, if I turn up to Belgium and British Cycling are like, what was that performance? Then that's that. I think I've made my peace with that. But I still really want to try."

But my word, it's exhausting. Hannah's just been to Kwik Fit to get her tyres fixed, and she's so fatigued from all the training and work that she forgets her own phone number, and then forgets the word for the little rectangular yellow thing that you have on the back of your car that has the letters and numbers on it. And it's a bit rubbish, because everyone's memory goes a bit when they get older, but if Hannah's too old to still be living with her parents, she's much too young to be losing her mind. It's hard.

"I've committed to this for so long now," Hannah says, "and sometimes it just feels like you're shouting into an abyss, and that nobody sees, and nobody cares, and you're all on your own, and it's just so much. It's so much to do alone."

*

LAST CHANCE

A few weeks to go before Belgium – Hannah's last chance to turn heads at British Cycling before they select the team for Tokyo – and she's in tears.

The trike that Mike Ellis has been working on for months and months and months is done, and it's brilliant. It's so much easier to corner with – and that was the thing, Mike had specifically designed it so that it would be better for corners. It's light, it's aerodynamic – for a trike, at least. It's beautiful.

"I don't know if people really get how emotional it is for me," Hannah says. "There's so many amazing cyclists who get upgraded bikes every year. It's not a big deal. But trikes basically haven't been engineered, at all, for about fifty years. This is historic."

She's not going to get to ride it.

Mike wasn't, it would seem, planning to tell her. Second-hand, Hannah had picked up that the trike was ready, and so she messaged him to ask if she could test it in Belgium, and he said no, and that's about it. He's giving it to David Stone.

"It's just crushing," she says. "He's got this amazing trike, and he's known me for a long time, and he knows how much I need it.

"I just want to ride it in a race. I want to beat the other girls, you know? I mean, sure, that doesn't necessarily mean I'll get to Tokyo – but this is different engineering. He's basically solved cornering – and it's just crushing that I will never know what that feels like."

She's not going to beg. She does still want one thing, and that's some closure – if Mike's not going to let her have the trike, then so be it, but she'd like him to say it to her face, and she'd like him to tell her why; but if he doesn't, then she'll move on, because what choice is there?

"It's not like I would have done anything differently," she says. "If there's no way that I can make him let me ride the trike, then that's it.

"In the end, this isn't actually the sort of thing that makes me really anxious. What makes me really anxious is when there's a form I need to complete or something like that, something specific I need to do, and I need to know exactly how and when I need to do it.

"There's nothing like that here. There are no actions for me. There's stubborn versus stubborn, and he's more stubborn than I will ever be. I can even understand his decision, too, if I take myself out of it. It's his baby, it's his project. So I'm like, ok. Ok. Your loss. People will be people."

So Belgium; and Carol Cooke and Jana Majunke, what with covid restrictions and all, aren't going to be there, so she might still be in with a shot of making the podium. "I should at least be better than I was at the end of 2019," she says, "when I had that disastrous performance at the world championships and fell off.

"The problem is, I'm not there yet with my race trike. When I talk to my friends about the Mike trike, their reaction is to say, 'Well, at least you've got a trike that you know, and that you don't have to get used to.' But that's the thing. I don't.

"I just tried it out the other day – I've been working on it with a really nice mechanic – and it tried to tip me off a bunch of times. I have no idea why. Something's changed, and I can't work it out. I'm trying a few different things, and I'm going to go to Belgium and see what happens, because maybe I can pull something out of the bag, but right now this race trike feels alien. It feels so much more unstable than my training trike – and that's super rusty, because it's spent the whole winter battling the elements. So yeah, it feels like there are so many things that I don't know right now, and I have no idea what to do."

And if all that weren't enough, she's had her blood test results back, and she's got an autoimmune disease called primary sclerosing cholangitis, and she's going to need a liver transplant.

She'd honestly thought it was just what training with CP felt like – feeling fatigued all the time, battling brain fog. The GP had been concerned enough to want to investigate, just in case, and here we are – not quite a one in a million thing, but not what they were expecting, either.

Still, she's being allowed to carry on training and they're going to let her race; and a few days later she receives a phone call from one of the British Cycling sprint coaches who happens to have the same thing and managed to compete at a couple of Commonwealth Games with it – and what do you know, he's been to the World Transplant Games too – so that's a massive help. Paula Dunn's been in touch too, checking she's doing ok, and meanwhile her performance is coming back. There are graphs showing that she's back up to her personal best powers, and she's squatting some serious weights.

So off it will be to Belgium. They're not allowed to go through France because of covid, and for one reason or other the only spare member of staff who can go with her is the director of Scottish Cycling, David Somerville, and so for what might be Hannah's last ever trike races, they're driving her car over to Hull and taking a ferry.

Last chance to make an impression, last chance to get to Tokyo. "And then," she says, "for good and bad, I'm finally going to be free."

*

BELGIUM

Well, now.

The race trike is a write off. Hannah does a practice time trial, and she can't steer the thing. No idea what's wrong with it, she's tried to change pretty much everything and nothing's working, and so there's no way it's taking her round a race like this.

Right then. I've been riding my training trike, she thinks, and I can handle it. So last minute, it's decided – Flash is going to Belgium, with a change of bearings, some upgraded wheels and that's about it, not even pushing the boat out for any go-faster stripes. What else? A skinsuit from Endura, through a contact of a contact, and some advice from an aerodynamics specialist.

So that's all positive, but going into the competition, for about ten days beforehand, she's not doing great. Can't eat. Can't sleep. She's desperate not to make a fool of herself, desperate to go out – if this is going to be it – with a bang, and when on top of that there's also this liver thing to be working through, the expectations are being dialled back. Just try to get through it. Put one foot in front of the other.

There's a guy called Ali Jawad, who's a para GB powerlifter. He's gone through some health issues too, and Hannah sends him a message to say look, how do you do it? Because I feel like crap. And he tells her, right, you just have to compartmentalise. Where people would normally try to process things, he's like, don't process it now. Process it after the Games. Don't be sad now. If the medical advice that you're getting is that it's ok to race – and that is what they're saying – then just put that first.

Then a family friend who lives in Glasgow, she's 22, just finished her degree at Glasgow University, gets in touch to say Hannah, I really need to get out of the house, can I come and help you out in Belgium, and in all this time, thinks Hannah, no-one's ever actually *offered* to go to Ostend with me – which makes a fair bit of sense, to be honest, it's not exactly Majorca – so yeah, why not?

So off they go, Hannah and her friend Carmel and David Somerville, "and straight off," says Hannah, "I just felt this positivity radiating out of me. That's something that I haven't felt in a long time – and I just thought, oh, that's what the pandemic's been doing to me. Because I love travelling, and I love being with people, being with a team, a high performance team – even if it's one of your own making. I live for that shit. That's basically why I work so hard to set up these races."

Because of covid, there's a million tests to get through. There's a PCR[3] test before leaving the UK, and then they get to the ferry at Hull and there's a private LFT[4] that they do there. A couple of days after getting to the race hotel, there's another PCR test – and then an LFT before they leave the competition, and another one after that because the first one gets rejected because of something to do with what was and wasn't and should and shouldn't have been written on the little bit of paper and so they have to stay an extra night in Rotterdam because admin but anyway... back to the racing.

"I've always had great nights' sleep on camp," says Hannah.

---

3. Polymerase chain reaction – poke the swab in, swirl it around, try not to gag, send it off to a lab which checks for Covid-19 RNA and lets you know within a day or two.
4. Lateral flow test – see above, except that it checks for antigen proteins and gives results in around half an hour.

"Life is so much, for me, and racing is an escape, and always has been. Catered accommodation, and having people help you out on all the stuff that you struggle with? It's luxury.

"But then it gets closer to the time trial, and just before the race I feel like I want to throw up. Everything's riding on it. I'd been told a week before that I definitely wasn't going to the world championships, I'd just been told I had this life-threatening condition. But then as soon as we got going, I was in my happy place, and with a trike that I could control."

Carmel and David have done a brilliant job, everything goes like clockwork to get Hannah to the start line, and she's the first off, with Monica starting a minute behind her. Ok, she's thinking. Monica's going to catch me, but I'm not going to let her go.

And Monica does catch her, but Hannah hangs on for a fair chunk of the race, and even closes the gap a bit; and Jill pulls back the best part of a minute over the last few kilometres to finish ahead of Hannah too, but that's about it. Hannah's not coming off the back of vulva surgery this year, she's a bit more aerodynamic, and she crosses the line about two and a half minutes quicker than her time around the same course back in 2019. She feels in control, she feels fast, and yeah, there's no Carol, and yeah, there's no Jana, but you know what? It's still a fucking bronze.

Chill, rest, then go again for the road race, and wouldn't you know it, the day dawns and it's basically Glaswegian. Blowing a gale. Four degrees. Sure, Hannah normally likes the heat, but the Americans are *hating* this.

There's a hold up at the start too – a crash in the men's race so everyone has to be tipped back upright or something, and you know what, this feels good.

Hannah's leading out on the first lap, and then there's these big windy straights, and there's a new rider in the race who goes on the front straight away. Fantastic. She's not going that fast either, this is perfect. Then the end of the first straight, and the new rider, a Dutch T2, just stops dead, and she won't go on the front. And Hannah's not going on the front on the way back either, and neither are the Americans, so it's the other rider in the race, a Greek T2 who's been knocking around the circuit for a while, who takes it up. No-one's really working, it's turned into a tactical race, so the pace is pretty slow, but the Greek rider's looking strong, and Hannah's tucked in behind her.

She takes the front for a corner. Technical section again. Come on, Hannah.

It's not entirely clear why, but she's starting to feel things coming together. She's so happy to be there, and Jill and Monica are so miserable about the weather.

The Americans take the front for the second lap, and Hannah lets a bit of a gap form so they have to through-and-off[5] together. It's a dangerous position – at any point, they could just decide to attack, but she stays in touch through the whole front section and the whole back straight, and then it's the third and final lap, and definitely time for Hannah to start doing some work.

The Dutch rider is still up there, but she's not doing it right. Hannah, Jill and Monica are working together now, through and off, through and off, but the new rider is riding over to the side, which is all very well, but in windy conditions means that she's doing about eight times the work of the women she's racing against.

But they can't shake her off, and then it's into the last few

5. When there's a small group of riders together, they'll all go a lot faster if they take turns at the front. So the leader puts in an effort, drags the others through in their slipstream, then ducks off to the right and rejoins at the back of the line. The next person gives it some, then off and round they go, and so on.

kilometres. Hannah gets in between the Americans so now she's behind Monica, Jill's behind her, and the girl from the Netherlands is back in fourth, and Hannah takes the front on the last hairpin, so then it's just 5k until the finish.

The new rider charges forward, she's got some power and she's doing her best to go but she's not getting away, and Hannah and the Americans wait and they wait, until with about a kilometre to go, Monica just launches.

With the long straight final section, the speed has been picking up, and picking up, and picking up, and suddenly Hannah's going at about 40km/h, and she's barely ridden that fast in her life and it's exhilarating. They've dropped the Dutch rider, Hannah doesn't realise it yet but they've dropped Jill too, and somehow Hannah's still got the energy to give herself a pep talk, and she's saying to herself over and over again, get gold. Scottie. Katie. El. All the big cycling women in her life. Helen Scott, Katie Archibald, Elinor Barker. They've got their gold medals, they've got them already. Gold. Get gold. Scottie. Katie. El.

Hannah's a sprinter. She's been a RaceRunning world record holder at 100m, at 200m, at 400m. She's built herself up into an endurance rider in order to stay competitive on the trike, but she's always been the girl with the need for speed, ever since she saw the picture of Gavin on his RaceRunner, looking so free.

Training's been hard to fit in recently, around work and everything, but when she's got out, she's managed to do bits and pieces. Sprint to the sign. Sprint to the tree. Beat that person, get there first. But no closed roads, nothing at this speed. She's done one competitive sprint finish as a trike rider – ever – back in 2015, at one of her first ever races. And here comes her second.

Surely Jill's right behind me? Make it over the line, make it over the line. You wanted a sprint finish, this is your sprint finish. This is your moment. This is your time. Surely Jill's behind me? Fuck, I'm going to hit her if I pop out now. Ok, I'm going to have to go, fuck me, this is like trying to get round a lorry.

One lane goes into two for the finish line, lots of cones. Cones?!?

"It was a miracle I was there, in so many ways," says Hannah. "So I was so happy, the whole time. I was so happy that I was racing. You know that really terrible, positive person that you just want to shoot? That was me."

She can't shake that off. It's been in so many ways the perfect race, and she didn't pop out in time and Monica crossed the line a wheel ahead of her and for a little while she's annoyed with herself, you know, gold was that close and you didn't get it and all that, but actually, what more could she have done?

Maybe British Cycling will disown her completely now, and maybe that's it. But you know what, Hannah, give yourself some credit. You've pretty much never had an opportunity to train with trikes, so how would you know how to sprint finish a trike properly, at speeds like that?

So when they get back from Belgium, she has a Zoom call with Scottish Cycling. There's a physiologist on the call, and Hannah's strength coach, and a man called Dave Daniel who's a sprint coach but has also become her de facto cornering assistant, and her performance lifestyle advisor Chris Volley, and David Somerville as well; and as far as they're all concerned, it's straightforward. For the next few months at least, we're going to support you, what do you need, what can we do?

So what can they do, and what can Hannah do? She's tried to hand in her notice at her contact tracing job, but her line manager is too nice and wants to do what she can to help too, so for now – and Hannah is going to try quitting again before too long – she's doing four-hour shifts a couple of times a week, which means that she's earning a bit of money, and it doesn't really get in the way of training. She's got a few hospital appointments coming up too, just to assess the damage that her PSC has done to her, although she doesn't really want to know how bad it is – it's more for the doctors, just in case it looks like she might explode on the finish line or something.

In the meantime, Hannah and David have emailed British Cycling, because they reckon that she's on the borderline for Tokyo selection, and a graph or two showing that her performance – 2019 aside – has been tracking in the right direction for a while might just do the trick. They can say that her metrics have been improving, particularly the shorter burst stuff, and that she's ticked up a few watts on the twenty minute powers – which means, in short, that her endurance has stayed the same or maybe improved a touch, and she's sprinting better too.

What's more – and they've touched on this as well – the course at the Paralympics is going to be hilly and technical, and every hilly race that Hannah's done, she's been getting closer and closer. What do they reckon she can realistically aim for? No more than bronze, maybe, in the time trial, but in the road race, it feels now like she'll be gunning for gold. She can get on Carol's wheel – why not? – and the whispers from the American and German camps are that they're only going to be sending one female trike each, so if that's the case, they're not going to be able to two-up her either; and she's seen Carol's numbers on Zwift and knows that if it comes down to pure endurance, then she's buggered, but if she can take it to a sprint, she can hit numbers that Carol can't.

Jana? She's probably the strongest climber of the lot of them, but maybe Hannah can stay on her wheel now, and then take her at the end. It's so good to feel excited again. She can't wait, she says. Just hoping, hoping, hoping to get the opportunity.

Eat, train, sleep. Eat, train, sleep. Sort out hospital appointments. Eat, train, sleep.

And Paula Dunn checks in – have British Cycling told you whether you're going to Tokyo or not? How are you doing, how are things? Which is cool, because whatever happens in terms of cycling, it feels like there's a definite future in sport for Hannah, now. The world championships in 2022? Yeah, for sure, why not? As soon as RaceRunning[6] is confirmed as a medal event, they're going to be working together, let's do it. "And it's just that," says Hannah. "It's just that. The promise of more competitions, with supportive, fun people. That's all I want – to do the work, and to be supported."

*

6. Or, to use the new name that it's given itself as of early 2021 as part of an effort to grow the sport internationally, Frame Running.

DECISIONS

In the run up to the European Championships in Varese, Jess's recovery seems to be going exactly according to plan. She's getting better, and she's pushing hard. In the double for now, working with Saskia Budgett while Holly's out of the boat for a bit? Cool, fine.

Although it does feel a bit odd, to be honest – a bit too much like she's just keeping the seat warm, even though as far as she's concerned, she's fit and healthy. What's more, for all that she knows that there's going to be seat racing afterwards, she also knows that it's Europeans, then either the final Olympic qualification regatta or the Lucerne World Cup, and then it's Tokyo; so if she's going to make it onto the plane to Japan, she needs to find her way into a boat sharpish.

So she's pushing for a race – which, after a while, is what she gets: a race against Holly, for the second slot in the double. Each of them doing 1500m on the water with Saskia and 1500m on the ergo, swapping halfway through so the person who did the ergo run first goes on the water second and vice versa.

Now hold on a moment, I just want to say, points out Jess, that that doesn't sound very fair to the person who's going on the water second. All very well to take a hit on your ergo run, but fresh person with a fresh Saskia doing a time, and then tired person and tired Saskia, doesn't seem ideal.

It's the best we can do, the coaches tell her. There's some men's singles racing going on at the same time, so we'll take how that goes into consideration too – tiredness, conditions, all that. Fine, thinks Jess. It's not how I'd like it, but I'll take it, because I'm going to make sure it's a coin toss anyway so it's not preferential, and for now, this is the best opportunity for a race that I'm going to get.

It feels important. Because yes, there's going to be testing for the final seats after the Europeans, but it looks like Jess will be going into that testing as just about the only person not to have raced, the only person not tuned up with some recent exposure to high intensity performance; and she really doesn't want to be in that position if there's anything she can do to help it.

The build-up's not great either, Holly's allowed to do a bit more work out on the water, and then it's the coin toss, and Holly's going first, and they do all the racing, and Jess loses by two seconds – perhaps a bit less all in all, because the men's singles race was slower second time around too.

Still, she's done everything they've asked her to in terms of covid recovery, and she's feeling strong. Back at the start of the year, when she'd just come down with it, they'd told her not to worry, not to rush. We're going to be improving the boat until June, you've got right up until the announcement, basically. It's fine, don't worry, don't rush.

Europeans. While the others are racing, Jess goes up north for a bit and does some work, on instruction, on a dynamic ergo – which is meant to be a top-of-the-range training option, designed to encourage precision and posture, but she's never really been on one before, and her lower back goes into spasm part way into a session.

Back down south she comes, to see some multisport physios, and they think that the back spasming has happened because of tightness around the thorax, and one of them says that maybe it's something to do with covid – which is a bit of a surprise, because Jess is pretty sure she's over the covid now. But either way, the physio is saying it in a positive way – we can help you, it's not that your body can't do it, it just needs a bit more support, that kind of thing; and sure enough, her back sorts itself out within a week or so.

Europeans. The double wins bronze in a photo finish; Poland don't even make it to the A final in the quad, and Great Britain elbow their way ahead of the Germans and follow the Netherlands in for silver.

The first phone call she gets is about the double. It's Holly and Saskia, that's who they took to the European Championships, and that's who they're going with for the final qualification regatta; and that's kind of fine, but she's trying to ask about the quad too, and it's not sounding good. So am I, she asks, going to get another opportunity to race for a seat? Yeah, we'll see how it goes. Depends on performance, but yeah, you might. Ok, she thinks, at least I've still got a chance. I mean, I don't want to be strung along all year, to then get to the point where I haven't had an opportunity.

But something doesn't feel right. She messages. She waits.

They call again later.

Yeah, you're right. You're out.

*

MY WAY

And for all that this is the day that, after seven years of training in the senior squad, she's learnt that she's not going to the Olympics, one of the first emotions that strikes Jess is relief. Relief that she's not going to be strung along, and a feeling that she's taken control a little bit.

She could still be there, as it goes, still be trying to scuttle around for a spare seat. But right now, she feels like she wants to get as far away from all of it – the politics, the people, the system – as she can. Right now, to be honest, she feels like she's been messed about on the basis of one Europeans result, that seems to have just locked everything down.

It's not, to be even honester, like all of the other scullers have been on top form, and Jess has just been the odd one out, with her covid and what have you. Everyone's had injuries, everyone's missed training all over the place. British Rowing don't even send a quad to the final world cup. Is there an appeal that she could put in, then? Well, yes – kind of. "I feel like I deserved more of an opportunity," she says, "but if I were to appeal, what would it be based on? I haven't got a solid result behind me this season. I haven't actually raced properly, with covid and with my rib injury before that. If you look at it that way, I haven't got much of a leg to stand on."

And so she's sad. "I've got one of the best ergos on the whole team," she says, "and I've been part of the quad project for years, so I clearly don't scull that badly. I'm just sad about the situation, because I thought if you worked hard, and you tried your best, you'd get somewhere.

"In my life, I've had loads of 'life's a bitch' kind of moments. Like losing my dad, and my uncle, and all of that.

"You know when you're a little kid, it feels like you can do anything in life, everyone's equal, everyone's got all the same opportunities. Then you go through school and you start to see other people getting ahead because of where they were born, and who they know, and some of your friends get cars bought for them, and stuff like that, and bit by bit you start to think, oh, yeah, life's not actually fair. I think sport was the last area which was like, if you just work hard and you get your head down and you're the best, then no-one can argue with it."

Jess goes off to somewhere in Harley Street, to have a lung function test which shows that her lung capacity is 134% of that of a normal person, and that it's working at 115% efficiency. She does a fitness test at the Institute of Sport, Exercise and Health, and all the doctors are asking, how are you, are you still not feeling great after your covid? No, she says, I feel fine, I feel really strong. Oh, that's good, they say, not really believing her at first, but then she does the fitness test, and she's broken a lab record. Wow, that's incredible, they say. You're an incredible athlete, that's really, really impressive. And that makes Jess feel a bit better, because it just shows how all her hard work has paid off, and that she's in really good shape.

During the exercise tests, they find something slightly odd with her heart. We're not completely happy with this, they say, because we've seen a footballer that had the same trace, and he had covid but felt absolutely fine, but then we found out through the MRI that he had inflamed heart cells. So Jess – who's obviously got her family history of heart problems – is like, ok, I guess you have to do that. They do an MRI, put dye in her heart and everything; and a week or so later, the results come back, and yeah, it was nothing.

"I think at some points over my seven years in the team," Jess says, "I've probably gone too far to sacrifice happiness. I mean, no-one's life is easy, sometimes things are really hard and you just have to get through, but this has blown a lot of things out of the water for me that I always thought were just a given. It felt unequal. It felt unfair, and if that's what sport is, then frankly, I've lost a lot of respect for it. At the moment, it feels like I'm not really sacrificing much any more by taking myself away from it all for a while, because the Olympics means so much less to me now.

"But I still really love just getting on the water. Even on my darkest days at the moment, as soon as I get on the water, I can't take the smile off my face. I just love rowing. I love training – I get in really bad moods if I don't train, or I don't exercise. I won't sacrifice anywhere near as much family time or happiness for the sport any more, and I want to finish my engineering degree, that's really important to me; but I think I do want to carry on with the rowing, doing what makes me feel happy.

"And I think I just won't ever get to an Olympics if I can't do it that way. I'll just stop. That's what I'm using the next few months for – to work out where I want to train, how I want to train, what programme I want to do, how I want to balance my life better. Try different things, because I don't want to just go straight back into the same system that I've been in for so long. I'll have to work out my own way.

"I'm thinking of going back to Leander for a bit to start with. I need to change my training programme, because I obviously can't just do the generic one. I need to make something more bespoke to me and my needs, rather than going through the normal programme, and breaking something, and going back to it, and getting ill... I can't keep doing that. It's not good for my body, and it's not good for my mental health either.

"And I need more flexibility in my life. I've done seven years of working the best part of six days a week, and having a day, a day and a half of trying to sort my life out, or trying to fit my life around that. And it's impossible, because you can't organise your life, and you just get stressed, because everything's closed when you're off. It's just a nightmare. I'm an adult, and I can take time in my day, as long as I get all my training done. So I need to take more control. Not everything fits around rowing, now. Rowing will have to fit around other things."

She needs space. She doesn't have any problems with any of the scullers personally, she doesn't hold any grudges, but she's going to need a bit of space while they're doing Tokyo. She might do some fun racing, though, and frankly she's pretty happy in herself, with her life, with Adam. She's still going out doing stuff, seeing all her friends – she's not maudling around, but going into Caversham's really difficult at the moment. Whereas at Leander, she knows that she'll enjoy just turning up every morning and getting out on the water.

What of – not regrets, perhaps, but the path not taken? "If I hadn't got covid? If I'd been selected? Yes, I think I probably would feel more satisfied on the rowing side; but I do still feel like I've done my best, all the way through. It's unfortunate that I got covid, but I didn't flout the rules, I didn't do anything stupid, and over the past few months I've done everything that they've asked me to, at the right intensity levels, all that.

"And you know, over the last seven years, I've still achieved quite a bit that I'm proud of. Even though it doesn't say it on paper or anything, I know what I've put into that quad project, and I'm still proud of what I've achieved, and of the enthusiasm and excitement that I put into it all.

"I still know where my medals are, too. I'm glad I'm a good rower, as well as just enjoying being out in a boat. To be honest, as soon as this all happened to me, I promised myself that I wouldn't let anyone take my happiness away. I haven't done anything wrong, and I haven't lost, and I haven't let myself down.

"I mean, I could regret some of the sacrifices I've made, in terms of getting nothing out of it at the end. But then again, that's not my personality. I would have more regrets if I hadn't sacrificed all of that, because then I would have blamed it on that, do you know what I mean? But I do know that if I make those sorts of sacrifices again, I'll be making them for myself."

So what next? In the immediate future, training pretty much as normal, trying to set up something in a single and make that go as fast as she can, sure. But otherwise, some different stuff. Some engineering work experience, maybe, a bit of normal life. Get her motorbike licence, perhaps, while the Olympics is on – not to really do anything with it, but there's something healthy in the occasional "eff you", no?

She won't be quitting rowing. "I love training every day," she says, "and also, I don't feel like I've got the best out of myself. Obviously my biggest weakness is training consistency – I just get injured or ill, and I have done ever since I came to Caversham, so I need to use the past seven years of data on my training and work out a programme that works for me.

"Things like cutting back weights sessions – I don't actually need to be as strong as I am – and then using that time to loosen off, because I just get so tight. Find out what kind of mileage I need to do. I've not got a specific weakness in terms of fitness or endurance or power, it's just that I need to work out how to keep my body loose and stop myself from getting injured, stuff like that. And then, if I can make my single go fast enough, and I can see that as a project, then I'll keep going at that. If I can't, then maybe I'll try and learn to sweep."

Detachment. She doesn't watch the final Olympic qualification regatta, where Holly and Saskia finish third, out of the qualification places. Frustration. "Even though I feel like I've been badly treated," she says, "I still want the quad to go and do well. I don't want it to come to nothing, after everything I've put in. Even if it isn't me doing it. Will I keep an eye out for their result when Tokyo comes round? Yeah, I don't know. I'll see how I feel."

We've come all the way back round. Five years ago, Jess sat outside the Crowne Plaza in Reading, feeling like she was an engineer who was still doing her hobby. World championships, world cups, injuries, sacrifices, a twice-deferred degree... and now the next bit, which will be about finding something that reflects who Jessica Leyden is now. There will be rowing in that, and probably competitive rowing in that, and maybe Olympic rowing in that, but now there are lines that she's drawn, sacrifices that she's learnt that she's not willing to make.

It's not really about what's wrong or what's right. If it hadn't been for covid, if she'd stayed in the boat, then she'd have been getting so excited now. But on the other hand, it seems like you can have a realisation like this, and you probably can't ever really go back the other way.

She'll keep rowing, she'll keep pushing, she'll keep making sacrifices; and if she makes it to Paris 2024, or LA 2028, they'll be some of the most special days of her life. But from now on, she'll be doing it on her own terms.

*

TODAYS; AND TOMORROW

It ends, as it began, with an email.

Hannah's been pretty chipper, things are going well with Scottish Cycling, she's managing to catch up with some of her Olympic friends and they'll be heading off to their pre-Games holding camp soon, so that's cool; and British Cycling confirm their Paralympic selection process, and all of a sudden it's the week during which, at some point, they're going to tell everyone whether or not they're going to Tokyo.

Hannah's convinced herself that it's going to be the Friday before she hears, and it's messing with her mind a bit on the Monday and Tuesday, and on the Tuesday she goes off to the cinema with Helen Scott. And they're chatting about stuff – what they thought about the film, mainly – and she gets home and turns her phone back on, and there's a message from Karen Darke.

To say hey, are you ok?

Oh.

Shit.

It's a pretty standard form email. You haven't been selected for Tokyo. If you want to appeal, this is what you have to do.

So she appeals. Not with any great hope of success, but she believes quite strongly that not only is she on par in terms of medal potential with a few of the women who've been selected, but also that there was scope to add on another slot to the roster, so they wouldn't even have needed to give one of the others the chop. So she puts in her appeal, and she'll wait and see what happens. In the meantime, David Somerville checks in, makes sure she's doing ok, and she speaks to Paula Dunn. It's good to hear some friendly voices.

"The overwhelming emotion is actually a profound feeling of grief," she says. "It's a really profound feeling of grief. Exactly the same, in fact, as what I felt when I lost Janice, even though they're completely different situations. And it's funny, because I've had so much grief over the past few years. Grief over Janice, and over having lost two of my friends when they were just 23 and 31. So I know what it feels like.

"It's like my soul has dropped out of me, you know? I believed that I was good enough, finally. And I was. I am. Finally good enough, and it was all coming together nicely. I'm in such good form, and I was ready to win that gold. To have that last sprint finish of my life, that last race.

"It feels like they've picked such an able-bodied women's squad, too – relatively speaking – which is infuriating, when the whole point was me getting on TV, to show that wee young girl with CP who's out there watching that people with spastic diplegia can participate in the Paralympics. And now that's not going to happen.

"What does this mean for the future? Well, I have to wait until after Tokyo, to see if RaceRunning becomes a Paralympic sport; and then if it does, I'm going to hop right on that programme for the next three years. And I'm going to get that gold.

"But in the meantime, what do I fill my time with? I've quit my job, so suddenly I've got to face life, and that's scary. I don't have a partner, I don't have my own home, I don't have an income. I don't have a PhD in Australia. And I have to live with this grief that I'm feeling – although I do know that at least that will pass. One foot in front of the other. Just get through today. Today. Today.

"I've stuffed my existence with friends. I've got such powerful connections, a proper support network, here in Manchester. I've made a new trike friend – a woman called Harrie Larrington-Spencer, an activist who's trying to make all cycle paths accessible to trikes. We're talking about how we're going to get Andy Burnham, the mayor, and Chris Boardman on board in terms of trike accessibility, and we're going to change things... I mean, hey, we talk about a lot of stuff, but both of us are quite ill, so who knows. But I want to do that."

The appeal fails. British Cycling send her one last email about the extra spot, setting out the reasons why they've reached the decision they have, and she doesn't actually read it straight away. Because after all of this, after everything that's been going on ever since the ski jump to Rio and the racing and the camping trip that became a cycling trip in the Hebrides, it's time for a break.

Try to see her father in Spain, once the covid travel restrictions allow. Perhaps do some adapted surfing. Rest. Maybe join a clinical trial, to try to cure the disease that might kill her.

You know.

Life.

EPILOGUE

A NEW CHAPTER

I'm not sure what we were expecting, the sunny August afternoon in 2016 when I first met Jess and we talked about Rio. I mean, it could probably go without saying – even if I'm going to say it anyway – that we weren't expecting a pandemic, and months on end during which nobody could leave their houses, nobody could do any proper training, and it wasn't clear whether the Olympics and Paralympics would happen in 2020, 2021, Tokyo, or not at all.

To look back now through the Belgrade rain of 2017 is to see four soon-to-be world championships medallists, of whom only one will make it to the final selection four and a bit years later. In between, Henley, with the Dutch and the duck. Silence on the WhatsApp group and trouble in the boat. Concussion, upheaval, Thommo and Jürgen. Rehab, a whole string of missed sessions and trials, rib injuries, so many rib injuries, and through it all, a rock solid commitment. Our Olympics! Selection for Tokyo, even, just before the whole thing got postponed for a year because of a virus that went around the world and ended up right back at Jess's front door; and with that – gone.

Could this new quad they've put together – the only boat that Jess has really known throughout the Olympiad, this Mathilda and Charlotte and Lucy Glover and the latest up-and-comer, a Northern Irishwoman called Hannah Scott – could it do something special too, do what Jess believed that she could, and win an Olympic gold in Tokyo? Yes, of course it could. Will it, without her? Maybe – although it's a brave person who says that it's definitely got a better chance. Is it right? That's not the right question. It is what it is.

And Hannah? Was Hannah expecting to spend so long feeling so far away, and then to come so close? Did she not have plans, and targets, and ambition, and talent and drive and desire? Did she not do the very best she could, with some of the best coaches and support staff around, with Storey Racing and new saddles and the small box filled with steam?

And for all of that, the times, so many times, when it was falling apart – major surgery, and isolation, and money worries, and doubt; and in the middle of it all, Janice.

Could she have stuck with John, stayed with Gary, sucked it up for Sarah? I mean, some would have done. Would that have been the answer? Perhaps. But if it had been, then maybe that's not the right question either.

They've both made – not mistakes, it's not a question of mistakes – but decisions. They've sacrificed a lot, and there will be things that they've missed that are gone for ever. They've changed – and of course they have, because what sort of person were you, five years after you were twenty-two? With the pandemic year, with the *pandemic*, with Janice, with Jess's uncle, with John and Gary and Scottie and Carol and Hans-Peter, with Holly and Mathilda and Charlotte and Beth and Melissa and Zoë and Thommo and *everything*, they're different people now.

And yet – and here's the thing – they're not. They're both

still the normal, brilliant, straightforward, incomprehensible women that, day after grey day after grim, painful day, roll up their sleeves and say right, Paris 2024, LA 2028, what have you got for me now? They are the women around us, the every-woman who is, quite simply, extraordinary; and they will just keep right on going, because it's what they do, and it's what they love.

Round the circuit, back to the start.

An engineer who's still doing her hobby; and a young woman with a need for speed.

Acknowledgements

Thanks, and a whole thicket of them.

Above all, of course, to Hannah and Jess. Both of them put a huge amount of faith in me, gave extraordinarily generously of their time and trusted me with their secrets. I hope that I have kept safe what I should, shared what I could, and done them service.

To those around them, who lifted up a couple of the corners – and in particular to Sharon Leyden, Margaret Owen, Helen Scott, Karen Darke, Katie Archibald, Ian John, Robyn Mawdsley, Gavin Drysdale, Melissa Wilson, Zoë Lee, Mathilda Hodgkins-Byrne, Gary Brickley, Holly Nixon and Beth Bryan.

To the team at Unbound, who took all sorts of chances – on me, on Hannah, on Jess. Particular thanks to Xander, whose early enthusiasm for this project helped get me through some extremely difficult days; to Anna, who was exceptionally patient with some incredibly stupid questions; to Mark for his brilliant design work; and to Julia, who understood.

To everyone who pre-ordered, and got us over the line to publication, from James to Steven. Particular thanks to Claire Eadington, whose generosity of spirit, of time and of pocket knows no bounds; to Rehan, Adam, David, Adrian and Barry; and of course to Mr Pugs, who is just as much a part of this amazing family as his non-canine friends.

Thanks too (with apologies) to Hollie, and thanks to Colin and to Caroline Searle, without whom who knows. Thanks also to Nick Walters and to Neil White, for all your support, your efforts, your encouragement.

To Greg Price and to Sadie Flayeh, for always being in my corner; to my sisters, Madeleine and Stephanie, and to Rob and Martin.

To my wife, Helen, for holding everything together and for carrying me through the hardest of times – none of this would have been possible without you. To our children, Mackenzie and Ewan, with a promise that you will now have more of me.

And to my parents – my mother, Annette, and my father, Jeff – for, quite simply, everything.

Miss you, Dad.

Unbound is the world's first crowdfunding publisher, established in 2011.

We believe that wonderful things can happen when you clear a path for people who share a passion. That's why we've built a platform that brings together readers and authors to crowdfund books they believe in – and give fresh ideas that don't fit the traditional mould the chance they deserve.

This book is in your hands because readers made it possible. Everyone who pledged their support is listed at the front of the book and below. Join them by visiting unbound.com and supporting a book today.

Lorelei Bere
Peter Boydell
Brian Browne
Nadir Burney
Nicola Cane
Juliet Clement
Martin Cloake
John Cramer
Amy Davies
Dee Doku

Daniel Eastment
Darren Fitch
Sadie Flayeh
Julia Foord
Tom Fordyce
Phil Gillman
Rhona Glazer-Munck
Ibi Gowon
Siwan Griffiths
Hilary Hall

James Herring
Rebecca Houghton
Dan Kieran
Robert Lomax
Emma Longbottom
Katie Lynch
Katie McCulloch
Steven Melvin
Austen Merritt
John Mitchinson
Suzanne Montgomery
Sarah Mossman
Husain Mukadam
Carlo Navato
Shani Page-Muir
Moin Parkhetiya

Jon Pavitt
David Penson
Martin Pickup
Justin Pollard
Tanya Preston
Geoff & Karen Ralph
Barry Reardon
Jenny Reynolds
Johanna Seingry
Dovlet Seyidov
Margot Shepherd
Tom Van Klaveren
Michael Verney
Guy Wheeler
Megan Whewell
John Witt